radiant danse uv being

radiant danse uv being

a poetic portrait of bill bissett

edited by

Jeff Pew & Stephen Roxborough

a blewointment book

NIGHTWOOD EDITIONS
ROBERTS CREEK, BRITISH COLUMBIA
XXVI

Nightwood Editions
R.R. #22, 3692 Beach Ave.
Roberts Creek, BC, Canada V0N 2W2
www.nightwoodeditions.com

Cover design by Milo Duffin and Stephen Roxborough
Front cover photo by Duncan Horner
Back cover painting "self portrait in may" by bill bissett (2004)

Nightwood Editions acknowledges the financial support of the Government of Canada through the Canada Council for the Arts and the Book Publishing Industry Development Program (BPIDP), and from the Province of British Columbia through the British Columbia Arts Council, for its publishing activities.

Printed and bound in Canada.

LIBRARY AND ARCHIVES CANADA CATALOGUING IN PUBLICATION

Radiant danse uv being : a poetic portrait of bill bissett / edited by Jeff Pew & Stephen Roxborough.

"A blewointment book."

ISBN 0-88971-210-7

1. bissett, bill, 1939- —Poetry. 2. Canadian poetry (English).
    I. Pew, Jeff, 1963- II. Roxborough, Stephen, 1953-

PS8287.B575R32 2006   C811'.54080351   C2005-907826-X

for bill

Contents

we dont
know as
much as
r pomes

–bill bissett

dere frenz uv bill bissett,

We had a poetic idea. It was endorsed by lunarians. Now we ask for your earthly participation.

The Idea: We noticed each time we talked to bill bissett we learned something about ourselves. We listened to him and he inspired us to write. Sometimes we wrote poems about him. We imagined he must have the same effect on other poets. We thought, why not collect poems about bill from his friends and fellow poets? We believe a range of insightful voices speaking about bill will create an intoxicating kaleidoscopic reflection-portrait almost as interesting and multi-faceted as bill.

The Endorsement: We presented the idea to bill for his blessing and this is what he wrote: "yr idea is brillyant love it fine totalee dont know tho if thers enuff around abt my work or me 2 make a book wud b way fun tho thanks a lot 4 yr brillyans raging happee trails mor as it cums in much love totalee n rockin love yu bill"

The Collection: We know bill is modest. Certainly we're not alone thinking he's inspired hundreds of electric/eclectic poems from friends all over the continent, if not galaxies beyond. We welcome you to send us your poem(s) about bill for consideration in this meaningful anthology. And, we encourage you to forward this email to as many friends of bill you think might want to write and submit a poem. We are looking for poems by poets, painters, songwriters, dancers, actors, waitresses, gas jockeys, bus drivers, movie house doormen… anyone who knows and loves and is inspired by bill.

Many xcellent and raging thanks!

Sincerely,

Jeff Pew and Stephen Roxborough
Projekt bill Editors

Introduction: danse uv th tru revulooshnary

Authentic revolutionaries admire change as an inevitable, ongoing dance. They welcome the strange and startling. They subvert false codes and bogus regulations. They help us understand the world as it really is: immense, chaotic, confusing, yet exotic, wondrous and full of mystery. They teach us to recognize change as a positive force, elevate our senses and embrace the remarkable as well as the mundane.

bill bissett, ahead of his time and somehow perfectly in time, is a true revolutionary. For many, bill is a seer, seeker, prophet, protester, magician, jedi, fool, jester, dada zen master, alien being, spirit guide, shaman, political conscience, shape-shifter, environmentalist, warrior, man-child mystic, trickster, bodhisattva, philosopher king and when needed, counter-revolutionary.

He meditates, power naps, and practices tai chi. He draws, paints, writes letters, emails, postcards and pomes. He scrutinizes cinema, reads auras and *Billboard*, cherishes Anne Murray, surfs cable news, welcomes strangers and comforts friends. He's the perfect passenger, dinner guest, confidant, movie companion and interview. He channels a direct line to the goddesses, sings lunarian to his monkeys and laughs with abandon. He's well-read, well-versed and well-informed. He holds his own on any subject, often reveals esoteric truth, yet in the same breath humbly states, "but i know less than nothing."

His favourite instrument is an encouraging heart. He offers kind words that invigorate and motivate. He lifts our spirits. Surrounds us with waves of positive energy. We feel good just hanging around him. bill's radiant, unconditional heart is the core of his art. Even bill musing about happiness rings profound: "can we

b lovd n blessd n totalee happee is that asking 2 much 2nite i know ium happee i can dew my work wch i love or putting it anothr way i can dew my love wch i work."

bill's loving nature and the respect other poets have for his talent creates a large, inclusive community. "frenz uv bill" from a wide spectrum of creative perspectives generously submitted poetic tributes from coast to coast. These broad-stroke panoramas and intimate portraits of bill, diverse in voice and style, share one common theme: love. It returns to him because he offers it so willingly to those open enough to receive.

Though revered in creative circles, bill remains a mainstream outsider. He's suffered the arrows of ignorance and has clashed with stubborn defenders of the status quo. He's been ignored and insulted in the towers of the self-important. He's been ridiculed and harassed by law and order, and most of all, by the narrow bias of fear. Undaunted, bill continues to live his life as art, break through barriers, stretch boundaries and subtly alter our cultural landscape.

bill understands the chaos of natural order. He knows our planet needs change, and shows us how to remove the lines we were told to colour inside. "ther ar no shuds wher i cum frm," he reminds. Does it have to be English? Paper? Justified? Horizontal? Right-side up? Create to destroy. Inspire. Teach. Transform anew.

He gives us a vast, liberating range of style, voice and concept to appreciate, ponder, and integrate. He challenges all to become better revolutionaries, dares us to dance with open hearts and fearless radiance.

poems

bill bissett

bare bones biography what els shudint i remember

collage makr i do poetry readings hitch hikd bak n
forth cross canada bout 7 or 8 times flew coupul a
times done sum time inside too playd with th mandan
massacre fr a whil hav bin welfare recipient tutor
fens buildr ditch diggr wintr works art gallry co-op
partnr the mandan ghetto help put out blewointmentpress
buks vancouvr startid with lance farrell nd martina clinton nd
others into vizual writing discovering *space* on a sheet
uv papr nd all yu can do with it nd th non gramatikul
line yeers uv poverty nd hard against th
correk line uv th ownrs – th faith to see how it can
be changes – once playd th student in goethe's faust
in halifax ths great halls bin lucky enuff to sit on
a few mountain tops wher i was born late 39 got out uv th
reserve air force thru brain damage was a teen age disc
jocky early paintr still am workd in garages very early
12 record store librarees staking buks sign paintr whn born i
weighed in at 12 lb 8 ozes pray that th world be mor open
as what is possibul that ther be less imperial isms ive seen th
sun rise and th amerikan empire set that th peopul share
diffrent undrstandings without one rule or sumwhun's
dominashun. one way is sure thru language sourse uv play
reverence pictures nd sounds, birds in th tree watr in th
earth whats in th sky sum times i dont know why. have
gone to a few dances at sum schools th professors didint
always believe it was me. ive never graduated from
anything. nu buks cummin out from blewointmentpress
by maxine gadd, gerry gilbert, bertrand lachance,
px belinski, bpNichol, ken west, nd others. th wheel nd
th drum uv the gestetener. thers a fire on th hill. love
nd th blessing to eat th coals in th hot snow.

je.17/71

The Nearest Star

"Hav u bin 2 sea th plants?"
he asked,
handing me an orange
a liquid joy
imports don't often retain.
I squinted closer into his
almost alien brightness.

We were talking
brain injuries, what passes for love,
and why the rich rule when there
are so few of them.

Deciding his question was
Metaphorical,
I realized: No,
I had not been to see the plants,
not for a very long time.

Suddenly we were skipping
through Allan Gardens,
two fairies noisy at the greenhouse door.
Some Metaphor.

And yet.

It was too late to go in
but he urged,
"My frend is heer from Vancouvr
fir just wun day.
Can you pleez let us in?
She sew needs 2 sea th plants."

He was lying,
I'm from Scarborough
and Kensington Market
but who wouldn't believe him,
smiling like that,
the universe green beneath his tongue.

The plants leaned towards him,
shoots forming when he spoke.

I leaned with them.

Illustration by bill bissett. Originally published in colour in *lunaria* (Granary Books, 2001)

Astral Twin
(as seen in a picture by bill)

Here's a person. You've seen him,
or her, before.
You think.

(If it was a him, if it was a her,
if there was a before.)
(If there is a you.
if there is a think.
Such boundaries blur in this landscape.)

He's made of lines, this one.
Just lines, no shading.
The space inside the lines is green
and purple and pink and yellow,
pastels of an odd sunset.

So is the space outside.
The same colours.
(It could be a sunrise.)

The eyes are open
in wonder or surprise.
They're star eyes.
The mouth is a little open too, lips parted
as if about to say

O look o look:
a miracle, a
muddy pond or dying cat or
silver tree or all three.

This is what you'd call a gaze.
Open-eyed rapture.
Open-mouthed.
Open-headed, because

This person has no top to his head.
Instead of a skull, instead of a skull cap
instead of an exposed brain
he has a circle of clouds.
You think they're clouds.
(if there is a you,
if there is a think)

or it might be a crown of mist
or it might be a soft garland,
or it might be an aureole of smoke.
Or it might be a joke about haloes.

This isn't a saint though.
Not him, not her.
Only you, looking
at your twin you looking
at you

Land a Cannot Can't

I live in Outland
Nobody's fool
Land no snap
On tool land this
Land is my/your hand
Land, no derivative
Spooled land, two
Bit dial-up
Land, no simian-cyborg
Ruled land; it's home.

We live in Outland
Take me as I
Land percuss perkiss
Land yes manhandled
Brand land but siempre
Fired heartland, ex
Pert kwizit
Weird land, rainbow
Vestibule land and I'm
With you here dear.

Margaret Avison

Playing Hookey

bill from BC
summoned bp
(who collected me)
from our day behind glass
to the sun and the grass
where he was – not when we
had a right to be free.

bissett's clear weather
was out there and we
smiled there together
a minute or two
planning somewhere to go
towards the end of the day.
Then bill wandered on
and we sunwarm went in.

There wasn't an end.
It's like that with a friend.

Phenhomona 3B

is 3 B
or not 3 B
the ?uestion

-

the 3irds
in the 3rees

and there!
　　　hidden under
two 3irds
in a bush

-

night is still
beside your hand
emptied by a 3ird

-

why not
2nd sight
with a 3ird eye?

-

Look out to C
and pasture, somewhere
3 rooks babble

-

on the cows
were 3
utterflies

Elizabeth Bachinsky

Only You

YOUYUOY
OYOUOYO
UOYOYOU
YUOYOUY
UOYOYOU
OYOUOYO
YOUYUOY

I've Never Seen a Mountain

I've seen moles, mole-shit
& the little piles of earth the moles push up when they dig their homes.

Are 'mole-hills' made of shit or earth?
In a short time there's no difference.

In another 100 years I'll be dead.
I won't be seeing mole-hills or mountains.

I want to see a real mountain, real soon.
I will cross the Rockies & visit bill bissett.

Douglas Barbour

a note for bill

that golden boy
chanting
for an elder poet's eye

those many years ago

she told us he
was different

we knew

it's everything
he did
was wow
(a) man
singing
slinging his stones

against the grey
goliath
grammar

the laws laid back
in time

Lake Worker

the People of Windsor were enthralled with bill bissett
they said "he will save our lake"
and it's there now

and the genii of rang swam in the summer's eye

Rhonda Batchelor

Nanaimo Confession – 32 years late

It's '72 and I'm wearing my hair in a white-girl afro and my skirts up to here,
all angst and attitude and insecure, Malaspina College girl
faking her way in the world. Drinking
at the Occidental with loggers and profs most nights,
I'm the intellectual Boho chick with a sensitive side.

I'm reading poems by guys like Newlove and Purdy,
stuff by McFadden, MacEwen and Lane.
I write some myself; have done since I was nine.
So when bissett comes to read I'm excited as hell.
This Brantford girl will get to hear bill.

A stoned-out friend has a dumb idea –
during the reading have someone deliver a pizza.
I don't know why I go along – knowing it's stupid, knowing
it's wrong. But I'm in the know when the knock comes to the door.
bill stops his chant. The host crosses the floor.

The delivery kid blinks at the room, sensing a trick.
Uh… somebody order a pizza?
The atmosphere is thick and there are
a few nervous laughs as bill looks around. The kid turns to go
but bill wants to know
Wot's on it?

Uh… just cheese.
bill digs out the cash. He gets the pizza
and the excellent last laugh.

snapshot

there is a smack of palm on dried gourd skin
as the spray-rain rattle fills the air
rich-toned voice and clear
a blue remembrance of Pyramid Lake
peyote warrior hot spring

a damp hug on a humid city day
when impossibilities overwhelm
box of rolled canvas splashed acrylic red
yellow winds, a single eye
the airport looming transcanada living

sliced oranges on a china plate
sweet citrus gentle spirit
enigmatic history a felt hat away
black and white west coast photo
in still frame, movie clip, a brain catalogue

where poems layer the atmosphere
like songs, like chants, like incantations
a body politic, the night dance
fresh spindrift of life and salt
words curled from the tongue
forming a column of energy, a splash of stars

a spirit, unfettered in the emulsion of the living

Karen Bissenden

bill Time

One of my volunteer jobs at the festival was to introduce bill
before his session and he said to say he had only been writing
for 7 years, and I asked "Well who was the guy with your name
I saw reading in 1976 in Vancouver?"

But he kept up the "7 year" theory throughout his entire lecture,
while explaining some of the roots of sound poetry, and everything
was "less than 7 years ago" or "a bit more than 7 years ago" or
if mentioning something in his own career "well that couldn't
have been more than 7 years ago"

and only when speaking of those various gods
that people channel did he say, "Well, I guess that
was definitely more than 7 years ago."

2 thousand milligrams uv pills a day cawses a lot uv shratching

my left foot is getting bettr thees antibiotiks ar sew strong ium breking out
in2 paroxisms uv itching they did say tho remembr we want 2 save th foot
yes uv kours i sd thank yu it was veree infektid by th time i went in with
it i went 2 an art opning uv a frend walkd th bleeding startid up agen i
think it was gud 4 me tho n will reelee help i will nevr spill scalding pot uv
hot koffee on me agen no wun els was heer i was in th kitchn 2 wch i now
entr wearing boots sew thers nowun 2 sue sept myself well its th itching
as almost 3rd degree burn cuts start 2 heel what am i supposd 2 dew just
lay heer scratching all day well th doktor she was sew nice n iuv lernd how
2 make wrap around gauze bandinage i keep th foot kleen undr cold tap
sevn times a day n put aloe vera on it thn th bandages no adhesv bandages
dusint let enuff air in it is getting bettr tho demain ium on a set all day
great xcellent i can sleep in tho its a late call sew thats xcellent dont yu love
it whn peopul say what wer yu thinking well 2 tell th trewth i was standing
ther by th scalding koffee funnul n karaffe n filttr all worreed abt th world
whil i was pouring th funnul tippd ovr did it help th world hmmm fingrs
2 th chin ancien jestyur n th thing 2 remembr is we want 2 save th foot
xcellent sew it looks like thats happning i hope cud we save th world xcel-
lent i know i wasint xcellent 2 go out yet i was sick uv hangin round inside
skratching sew i went out xcellent i think it helpd xcellent what dew yu
think th cuts arint bleeding much at all th swelling is down a bit okay sew
it hurts i think thats a gud sign i can onlee go sew manee dayze without
sumthing happning its bin that way 4 a long time i can go much longr b4
sumthing like ths happns tho thn i usd 2 b abul what that i a storehous uv
konflikting n awful n oftn xcellent memoreez n smtimes also konflikting
motivaysyuns all oftn way 2 linear n way 2 binaree 2 let go uv howevr best
bet oftn tho nothing is always yes sew thats veree xcellent tho i have no
knowledg n cannot know ths theoreez at all self portrait hmmmm agen
fingrs 2 th chin ancien jestyur o xcellent at first i kleend th burns with th
xcellent lens kleenrs lisa gave me evn th doktor sd that was smart thinking
xcellent veree soothing self elf lefs fel s lef or trait s p le sef hmmmmm

next time soons ium bettr ium gonna stay bettr evn longr sleeping undr th
brillyant stars at th bay uv fundee in nova scotia from wher i was reeding
in truro at th agrikultural college ther my monkees ar xcellent walking
home 2 th carlton arms hotel undr an xtraordinaree full moon from th
gallee uv amerikan art in chelsee anothr moon ths month full blu moon
th guide told me whn thers 2 full moons in wun month th changes we go
thru sew oftn not ours 2 undrstand onlee letting b cumming ce soir th sky
mooondee swirling clouds ovr toronto darkining sky all us tiny peopul on
th ground in iceland they ask psychiks n clairvoants 2 advise them whn
thers gonna b a road change re gentlee moving th large rocks as manee
invisibul peopul may live n love in them sew manee beautiful moons sew
manee brillyant stars th full moon ths month in toronto th 2nd in ths
month i sit undr n watch it moov n marvel n let go uv my self thredding
theoreez n breeth wher i am evn tho i dont know at last letting go 4 a littul
whil aneeway breeth eezee all th dances we go thru 4 2nite aneeway puttin
my foot up th painting ium working on shining n th singing pome n all th
frends radians evreewher sew manee lites we all ar can b thru i live in th
words n th images n wher ther is no word no image naytur breething being
ths nite dissolving changing in2 day thru th star filld galaxee can we know
ourself both and thers sew manee selvs 2 know b careful mooving large
objekts rocks hanging with elvs stars n treez breeth in th karessing winds
what dew we know how we know yu how we know yu how we know yu

bill bissett

Round & Round he goes & where he stops.

Round & Round he goes & where he stops
Round he goes & where will you find him, no
one seems to find him, round he goes & the
reading stops & he is gone before you have
begun to know, it stops & where is he, you
look round & round but he is gone & then
you stop, he is gone.

Round & Round he goes & round where he stops
the inky smudge of words of words yes of
words, oh of Words, oh smudge of words, a
smudge of words, round they go, in, & in,
you feel them inside each other, all inside,
round they go, till the letter, I'm thinking
of P, capital P, inside the P is a

Round he goes & knowbody knows. He sent me an
ap parition
er ap
parishioner, round to see me, a wrap
or issue, it was a
blew ointment for my rapt
derision, many years ago, round a
nineteen sixty too, where he stops, an
apt emission, to see, like it was a ghost of
smudgy ink, an inkster, & poet going round & round
inspiration, & instinctual apparition, this whole
thing goes round & round & isnt it ap parent &
isnt it a mazing that round it goes & right here
it stops.

Di Brandt

we all noh wot scientists hav bin dewing wth th embrioze

after bill bissett

they fownd out theez raging littel tighny pree babee cells R magik
they can beecum livr or brane or blud or toenales they can beecum
aneething human maybee eevn supr sumthing els

th inkorrekt thot pollees nevr liked th way babees R made
bi pimply adolescents 4 godsake wth poetree up thr branes
balling themselves silly in sweatee back seets uv cars noh
wun sd they cud th future in th hands uv pot smoking punks
n pimply grrls without car inshoorens ur drivers licenses

eye wuz thinking abt my frend eunice's frend in edmuntun
hoo has parkinsons n had 2 quit her nyce job selling
gud sekund hand klothes 2 happee neo hippee antee
globeliezayshun activists on wite avenoo

eye wuz thinking about my frend betsee hoo had 2 get pokd
wth staneless steel tools by sum wite coat in a lab trying 2
have a kid instead of swimming in th neon swimming
in th milk swimming in th neon swimming in th milk in th
sweet scented meadow behind the barn magikully lit up wth fireflies

evry wun dewing now wot big daddy apallo wth th shrivelld
dick sd frget about furtility goddesses wth beoootiful brests
beckuning across the see mum iz a petrie dish thatull bee five
thousand down dad a securitee code a plastik kard list uv
numbers on a screen

why put up wth upstart yung bluds wth jewelled sceptres nn
waving smoking sords when a turkey baster wll dew u kin
make th wimmin kleen toylets send the boyz 2 war

n now heer's superman in a wheelchare waving viagra at
th defecting dawters wth thr alarming nooly sprouted brests
hoo R chaned as uzhuwell 2 iron bedposts on steep rocks
n a junior investigator's tool box eye kid u knot a repro
ductiv plumber's kit 2 poke arownd in all thoze magikul
pree babees freeking out outside the woom for all th littel
boyz hoo wannabee astronots u kin order it on th internet
@ www.isscr.com

she hated all that staneless stele in hr soft crimzun parts
n finally quit n got a dog th dog fathred th kid eye guess
like th pissing littal yello dog in tom kings green grass running
watr all ovr th nissan th pinto th carmen ghia ha ha nnn
th soft pregnant hills uv professor alberta nnnn th red river valleee

my frend's frend duznt want the pree babees to be poked up for
her parkinsons kure sheez taken up vitamins n yoga everee
morning she meditates on green grass nnn liquid wayze
around th moon

my kids took ekstasee so thy cud keep up dancing awl nite
long at the group raves in trawno eye hope thy dont get parkinsons
iyum glad eye had them in a manger with a god insted of sum
dough boyz kemistree lab

th same geezers who made millyuns on birth control drugs
n screwd up th running watr n nervus systems n immunities
R making bilyuns on so called furtilitee n cancer
n parkinsons kures hey boyz n grrls iz this th kind uv whirrld
we want our ecstatic lives in th earthlee dimenshun reduced
2 artifishul apallonian virtchewel transacshuns uv plastik screens
n needuls n viagra daddeez stainless steel toobs n boles

Alice Breeze

Why Does Innocence Disappear?

masquerading as a human on earth he'd give you the wings off his back
as a human on earth he'd give you the wings off his back masquerading
a human on earth he'd give you the wings off his back masquerading as
human on earth he'd give you the wings off his back masquerading as a
on earth he'd give you the wings off his back masquerading as a human
earth he'd give you the wings off his back masquerading as a human on
he'd give you the wings off his back masquerading as a human on earth
give you the wings off his back masquerading as a human on earth he'd
you the wings off his back masquerading as a human on earth he'd give
the wings off his back masquerading as a human on earth he'd give you
wings off his back masquerading as a human on earth he'd give you the
off his back masquerading as a human on earth he'd give you the wings
his back masquerading as a human on earth he'd give you the wings off
back masquerading as a human on earth he'd give you the wings off his
masquerading as a human on earth he'd give you the wings off his back

The Rattle-Shaker's Song

What can the cheap-hearted say
        when the song thrives;
when the song will not be resisted;
when the song washes dishes
and then wanders outside, singing to Orion;
when the song meets the bear;
when the song walks the dirty street;
or when the song falls down invisible stairs?

This song is its own song,
        what every song should be.
Irresistible. Full of joy. Erupting.
This song is everywhere. You can find it
under the manhole covers. It has also
appeared in the house of parliament.
This song has been scurrilous, incoherent;
not in any language known to two speakers.
Sometimes it is only words. Only words?
Aw, if only women or men had the power of words.

Words? They don't even spell the way they sound.
What do they mean except the potential for magic?
Magic? That's the haunted melody following us
        wherever this song goes,
        and it fills us with delight
        when we learn to listen.

Elizabeth Brewster

Gold Man

I sit in my chair
with my hands and head full
of other people's poems.
Do I need to write too?

I drink rum and hot water
and am sleepy.
In my head a chant runs on
said by the gold man
about children and chains of gold.

No, I cannot chant too.

I come from a country
of slow and diffident words
of broken rhythms
of unsaid feelings.

Next time I am born
I intend to come
from a different country.

Allan Briesmaster

bill bissett

```
b i l l    b i s s e t t
 b l i s s    i s l e t
  s l i t    s t i l e
  t i l t     b i b l e
   t i l e    b i l t
  t i t l e    l i t
   t e l l s    i t
  b i l e    l i s t
   b    l    e    s    t
   b e l l    s i t s
  b i l l    b i s s e t t
```

Jim Brown

The bissetts

Ooljah says "my dolly doesn't grow
any older, Bijou knocked over the
egg things…"

bill tells me "they let people get famous
after they're dead, it's safe then, they
can't change anything…"

Martina is never the background
She says "you know I'm tired, Ooljah,
and you come to me with this great, big
question…"

We circle the attic room, the three of us,
putting bill's book together, collating
the pages and stacking them in piles
ready to be bound. Ooljah plays witches
with her cats at our feet

"Everything happens on december the first,"
bill sez. "The bulldozers are coming,
they are going to make a freeway
right through our house…"

Yeah, but, are they really gonna
make a freeway right through bill's house?
I wonder. Or, like,
a corridor for a commuter
train through Kerrisdale
and Kitsilano? Or what?

A freeway seems an
extravagance. I am just
getting to know bill
at this time, and I am
still applying logic
to every little thing
that is said and done

Ooljah has fallen asleep in bill's arms and he
carries her off to bed, to her room

Martina brings hot chocolate and we warm
our fingers on our hot mugs

Our circle begins again
I am aware of the three of us
moving in a dream
our shadows move with us
and bill's books pile up
at the end of the long table

Ooljah has fallen asleep
It is late
Tomorrow bill will take
the books to the binder
and on Friday
the bulldozers will arrive

Jim Brown

Th Very Tissues of Language

and hesitate along
and hesitate along th
and hesitate along th breath
two steps from th
two steps from th
two steps from th jail and
two steps from the sentence

> lean hollows/lean silences/lean
> together/lean on/lean on/lean in
> learnin/learnin/learning/learning

THE SUBJECT AND VERB OBJECT!

and hesitate along th
and hesitate along th breath th breath th breath
and two steps from and two steps from th jail sentence

ANGELS OF MERCY BETRAY US

> and thou shalt not and thou shalt not and
> thou shalt not and thou shalt not and thou
> shalt not and thou shalt not and thou shalt
> not and thou shalt not and thou shalt not

FOREVER'S A LONG LONG TIME, BABY

> lean, lean, lean
> it's never what it seems

buffalo bill's bin busted i guess
cause his grammar's not as good
as it shud be, cause he wears
a funny hat, cause there's gonna
be a war in this town sumday
cause there's a war everywher else
and what's so special about vancouver
and what's so special about
and what's so special

y'learn to live
an then you turn around
its all gon by, time
to look again

down to the very tissues of language down
to the very tissues of language down to
the very ISSUES of language down to th
very issues of language down to th very
issues of language down

"what we have here is a
failure to communicate"
Paul
New
man

th judge again
I sentence you

THE JUDGE WAS EATING FUDGE

I sentence you
i e o u
and some
times y?
i eo u

he's gone to pot
as they say
from drinkin too much
fear

the judge askt me
why i did it – how
th hell did i know
y?so they sent me
to this psychiatrist

Jim Brown

                              Y?he kept sayin'
                              & i kept sayin'
                              i don't know, no
                              i don't no
                                             this black umbr
                                             ella,it keeps
                                             th rain out
                                             and th brain
                                                       in

well dr bill
whats t'days operation?
when did yu first get
th idea for a noun
transplant?

                    sometimes dont ya just feel
                    like gettin a little wet?
                    i mean soaked

i think we better fix
our sentences up/the
motion was defeated
by the politicians
all in a row

                    democracy was a good thing
                    until they discovered they
                    could lie and just as good
                    as tell th truth

                         that
                         jordan
                         isamight
                         ywideriver

they just teach
us his story so
we ull under stand
what its like to
be in jail

42

amansamansamansamansaman
amansamansamansamansaman

hey you, you cant get
inta our heaven – your
hair's too long and
yuv got different
habits than we do

guilty guilty guilty guilty guilty guilty guilty
guilty guilty guilty guilty guilty guilty guilty

christ! you've said that
enuf times

okay so heres th key/watch me eat it

and then

you'll rot
by christ

here drink this hemlock mr wilde
and you too mr socrates and you
too mr pound, th policy of this here
city is carried out by our policy
force/i know i'm only an accountant
but i thot hippies were our biggest
tourist attraction mr mayor/stop/over/yes/sir
a rest a rest arrrest arrrrest arrrrest
there's a gap here somewhere better
look around men look around men look
around men – arrest that gap
or something's gonna pop

John Burgess

3 transmissions

01

we told him the entire universe
is made
      of the same stuff
the pbs special said the theory of everything
is strings smaller than physics can prove
bill acted surprised although he already
                knows this

standing outside his west end apartment
   an entire universe
    wriggling inside him

02

there are things we can fuse now
that we couldn't before

solder
melting across nano-circuits back-
spacing conjoined only as either or
keyboard mandating if not
0 then 1
   or as bill says
you can't double-strike keys anymore
spending a month setting tabs
and cauterizing possibility
before the screen   split

03

this one's about love
         the love
that wonders where love has
   gone
that loves all things
all moments
all people
      wonderful
love that doesn't do math
doesn't divide love into subsets

bill bissett

A herald a cumming rain vassal not withstanding. Goes like a monkey money fibbery finery and yellow is peaceful.

Milk a piston. Swing sets barter an outcry. Propel. Partake injurious glory for follow. Fallow crop a reinstatement statement state grace oblivious. Conversation encouragement will inform more than suppose. A credit card doesn't signify betrayal.

L'eave the term defined. Post-structuralism prolongs more symptoms if status requires vortex. If plaster is forthcoming why allow a feeder to be housed. Why not.

Wonderful wonderful an expression of piety. Dylan Thomas a propos but too facile. A life presence. Praxis. Nexus. Steamboat Willie. Cavalier functioning despite the time.

Steve Clay

bodhisattva in the meat locker

the frozen night
after your reading
december 1990
before the first gulf war
walking numb blocks
to my place on thompson street
for a cup of hot mint tea
you nodded to the stragglers
just making sure
one with his red hand
northwest corner of bleecker and laguardia place
you asked did he have enough to eat
someplace warm for the night

i was a little afraid thinking
what if he *didn't*

could i exchange
myself for another

you could and would
raging in
"th one blood stream"

Sexing the Page

                                    my derridean dissertation

        on the concrete poem
                        as rebus
        for the hermaphrodite body

                                was never so real as

the day my friend the archivist
                                with white cotton gloves
                                in the climate-

controlled vault

jerked me
                        (me)   (me)   (me)
                                                        off

all   over   the
                                        delicate

yellowed original

                    of bissett's

                    am/or

Leonard Cohen

dear bill

thank you
for leaving nothing out
fraternally
leonard

some memories and thoughts of bill

memories, flashbacks and histories are all imaginary in some way... it is hard to remember some things... it would be better if we could always live in the present moment in our minds because that's where our bodies are... to use the cartesian fallacy of a separate body and mind...

i first met bill in the caf at ubc at the theatre and writers and artists' table... my friend ruthy met him first... she said it was ok if i talked to him... this is 1961, but then there were all the other people there I'd like to talk about too... do we ever exist in emptiness by ourselves? veer off

bill bill bill bill billlb illbbilbilblblblblblblblbliiiiillllbbbibliiiiii bill fill hill rillskillbill

his first mother died when he was very young... he said she had been a saint... his sister, janie, still lived in halifax... he loved her very much... his father was "something else"...

we went to the black swan... bill worked in the library... so there is bill in 1962... how was he?... not great but great... even thinking about bill sounds like bill... maybe it is all just excellent... and an interesting experience... isn't?

how did bill decide to be bill?... just happened... gradually... attrition... a sense that this needed to be more immediate... a decision that the brain washing had gone far enough... imagine seeing *the manchurian candidate* 9 months before the kennedy assassination... well that was me but bill must have too as I think i remember him saying that he went to 5 movies a week...

he read everything... sartre, *the evergreen review*, roy daniels, aristotle, kant...

an excellent conversationalist... always completely broke... needing food... lots in the mind and not much in the stomach... a lot of people died but he survived and kept his goal in mind... a wide life but very focused, not much gets past bill and not much goes undone... how many books and how many paintings? obviously he can't be ignored when the histories come out... lives in the present but has to be remembered when they write about the past.

arthur cravan

bill bissett   re/view

think you know culture, you can't know
anything, knowing like water: you can
be in it (figure it "hot"), but not know
it. bill bissett doesn't use the figures
of other wo/men's speech, he reinvents
language, the value in this equation of
modern art the new wave of the mid-
sixties contributes. he's in it, loves the
feel. knows enough to realize coming
into other wo/men's mouths for clues
leaves you right where you already are,
knows enough never to resist. you first
get in to see how it'll feel, a thing way
more important all the way out as far
as you get to sea, than even the most
tasteful news from bygone mouths. that's
kinaesthesia. (forget I said that) the imp-
ortant thing is bill bissett. the importance
he's language. our language. meat marin-
ating in intelligence, the sound slapping
and pulling every which way, quenching,
drenching, cleaning, drowning (no) bearing
us deep inside the music of mother's voice
in amniotic swell, roaring, pouring, torrents
so cool our straining back at sun seems
less hopeless each new spray.

near forgotten phantasms

                buh bi   buh bi buh   bill buhba   bi ba bull ba
        buh bi   buh bi buh   bo bill buh   ba bi bull ba
            bill bi bull babul   bi-ba buh bullba ba
bi bissett   bubble   bill babi bubble bull ba
            bibble bi bubble booboo bi bibbl bo ba
        bo bill bi bulla   ba bi buh bi ba bull bah   bibbill bubull bo bill be bubble bill ba   ba bilt bi
bah ba   bull bi ba bo ba ba
                        bill build ee baba   bill bo bi ba bah bi ba
            built bi ba bill bi   ba bah ba bill aa ba
                bi bill di babble   build ee ba da ba bullba
        b bild bi bada   b bi b bild ee bo da
                bi bill di babble   build ee ba   da ba bullba
            bi bill bi builda   n bilt di baddi bullba
b build id babball   b bill bi ba bullbo ba
                bi bill did build did   buh bi billdid bullba ba
        b bill did builded   bi bo boo bull badaba
                b bild id bildid   b bilt a babibull bill
    ba b buh bilded   be bill did badda bo ba
            did boo bibuild did billdid bullba bo ba

bill did ya somethn the other night bill–
did ya somethn ya might still have bill did ya a pome bill
bill did ya lost thoughts n lotsa majikative recollections bill
did ya read the pome i fill did up with ya bill
did ya read the pome i buhbill did ya slip it off my head
build yer own imajikings whereabouts i bill did the bill pome
                        fill did up with yer
                            excellent
                                ize
                              zeeee
                        circuses in

                    near forgotten phantasms

Lorna Crozier

Winter Fox

On the road to the airport in Regina,
that fox we saw in the snow, thot-fox
you thot, and maybe it was
but that would mean we were thinking in
the same brain, our memories mixed,
and that red flare of pelt and muscle
seemed so real to me. God bless, you said,
thot or not, and meaning everything:
the sky, the car, the yellow grass whiskering
the snow, the fox soft-pawing his way
inside our brains, leaving trails for us
to follow anywhere, and bill, he's still there
though the real one might be gone by now,
off in someone else's poem, small wild thing
so beautiful and more so, to be blessed by you.

jwcurry

Review of *Th gossamer bed pan*

bill bissett
TH GOSSAMER BED PAN
(blewointmentpress, 1967)

j ocean dennie

annihilation uv p om

It begins conventionally enough.
Each line fits squarely with all the right stuff,
Rigid syllabilzation,
Refined word selection, diction,
Everything in rhythm,
In time, in rhyme.

Then something happy happens inside,
A waterfall of wonder washes over one,
And then some things matter less:
capitalization,
punctuation
     left justification
        all phrases having to be on one
                        line
                        kept
                        short
              what
                 ever
                      said
                so simple even children get it
            so concepts are toys
        worlds are playgrounds
     words then disintegr8
       in2 pure a wear ness uv funn
                loooook howwwwww silllllllly itt cud bee
                hullusinaysyuns dess cry bed fay th fah lee
       YOUS UV CAP IT ILLS REE KAP SHURD BE 4
  4 m   t h r one o w t th w i n d   o e
      con   creet   nessabandind
                                   4
                             gud
                      azzzzzzzzz
        wurds a peer
                           n d i s a p

Shedden

If, back in the hot city, trees are droopy green
fountains of frozen silence, what
of it? bill and I are on our way to the beach
leaving Shedden and the house you probably won't buy
flying giddy along Highway Twenty between fields
of brown earth and thin green lines that might be corn.

My materialist Russian car
can't keep up with our high talk of spirits
but faithfully carries our bodies through all four dimensions
down to the beach at Port Stanley, the burger palace
like the pavilion in *Stardust Memories*
fills us with light, gulls appear when we imagine
them, the green Erie horizon in all the windows.

At Hawk Cliff pairs of swallows fly from their holes
in the sand walls crumbling under our feet
embodied spirits of that place
in love with the air, they caress its many shapes
between us and the water and the sky.

Paul Dutton

oh bill bissett

1.

bill's listless.
he sits listlesslee,
set to sell belts –
set to toil to so sell;
set, too, to sell bells –
set to toll so to sell.

stilts?
bill belittles stilts,
lets stilts lie still.
his best bet is belts:
belts, bells.

bill's titles to islet lots – hot sites –
let bill sit still to sell belts, bells.
bill'll till his islet lots.
bill'll settle his islet lots.
it'll settle bill,
let bill sell belts,
sell bells.

2.

bill's bloo.
he ot to be, too:
he's beset bi lies he sees let loose –
the shittiest lies:
"bissett's hostile."
"bissett shoots hot bile."
"bissett's elitest."
"bissett's testee."

"libel!" sobs bill.
"it's so sillee," he hisses.

bill's blithe.
he's loth to let bile bite.
he blesses hi, blesses lo.
his bliss is boss.

bill's bliss is boss; bill's boss is bliss.
bill's so boss, so bill.
so be it.

Cathy Ford

the opening of the mouth ceremony

"dew / I have / to live / without / yr / beauty"
from *poems for yoshi* – bill bissett

(1)

fearless, peaceful we were sleeping geometries –
spirits sky released, five point encircled starshine, mirrored flat, transformatively earthed

an aligned energy as if streaked cosmic razing

warmed carved hieroglyphics, we folded into one another, to allow –
unmatched bodies like megoliths assigned to the galaxies, whirlygigged asymmetrical

ferocious sparks, envisioned truth a politic comfort, unremitting constellations

flutter giddy all round, exacting perfection, taking chance, we laid once all in a row –
copy drawing heavenly bodies on an imagined ground, picture thinking, shape shifting

inspirata coloured paint bits persuasion on skin, decoratively surfaced, seeking

(2)

initially, two wandered stones faced together, without gravity, proofreading enlightenment
your fierce beauty come back to this blue green planet, adamantly journeyed unbound –

here, by inclination, if not sacred accident, I actually met you

on this rising, gracious formality of relationship, dead souls reacquainted with breathworks
instruments transforming the heart, and lungs, afterbirthing, realizations now and then –

collating wonder, language not entirely translated, but trust freely deciphered

volcanic, once awakened, I made by orbital equinox hand for you alone
poet's dance rattle, repetition drummed from pink moon swimming scallop shells –

the certainty you remember everything, your sundance steps hum solstice wings
hinged enigmatic as your bluefield angelman, my obsidian black cannibal bird

(3)

above the avenue, gallery to the main pyramids, thought filled with teal springwater
canal cut deep into blown sand, seen from the first space satellites, camera obscura –

    take this picture, in our lifetime, infuse spirit lake reflected circular
    I see your heart in your eyes when we meet (again)

never alone, our acquaintance wrests memory outside, between sphinx paws, her medium
looking up at the tomb's ceiling, words alone sense this interior, his engendering –

    duarte, the davinci man, rilke, where soul goes, into the throat, having taken you
    in, your comet's tail trail imprinted on me, and never enough time, raven, river

measures of design, distance, the feminist orb speeds on its axis all raced
sex sounds undeniable, sphere's music gratefulness, lifeworks (eye) canvas –

    lapis lazuli, (ear) silver, no longer foolishly afraid, asteroid precious metal
    red passion ring, prayerful, apparent, your hand palms together with mine, this

feathered, third dreaming eye, abalone westcoast button cape drapes your shoulders
still, spillgate, ancient, handprinted, letterpressed, this constant (loving) directional signal –

    latitude, long, loyal, spoken word, where you are not lost, but found, this poetics
    (here) in me, once written, deep carved, fluid as heartbeat, radiant pulse, crow

when I first (be) held you, when I said, I have death on me
when you said, darlin (g), you just have to let it go, love –

(peace lily) above all, thankful, humbled pebble thrown into round moonlit pond, send a
postcard, just (once more) to hear your voice, another phone booth (seriously, heartfelt)

spell it write, shadow, read clear as conscious water, bliss, bill –

Patrick Friesen

white horse

a slide trombone
a bone and skin
the kind of beat
that isn't heard often
nor for long
in most places
out of almost nowhere
the slide of a voice
and a white horse
at full gallop down davie
a moving heart attack
a walking heart break
the motion of a heart
and nina simone
in his ear billy eckstine
that kind of attention
that focus beyond anger
but threads of it
still fraying the edges
of that slide of a voice
and not heroic
no saint
but all the listening
all the listening
and never asleep
all that willingness
to hold and let go
the willingness to die
that wide-eyed horse
riding west

bill is a book someone will do someday but

I.

With friends one doesn't really need to know everything about them. There is a fate in being known as "Bill" or "bill" as there is being known as Jeff or Maxine or Peggy-Sue, capitalized on or not.

Everybody has the great big brand wound of the name, the names, Names

II.

Th bill pomes
i don't know how to do
the bill poems all
pomes are to Sweet William
billy boy and billy-wielding mom or dad and the the dead who demanded
that in spite of impending whatever
poems
will
be done
oh old ballads, o
o
o
0
the Willy that wends through all our wanton ones
the true blue Bill that mans the white sails over oceans, lost, longed for, laughed with
the sails of the will
wanting
will
the bill that stands on a bird, the bill that comes and must
be paid out like the rope of the sails
the old singing ocean
our goddess
our origin
the will to keep listening, talking, reading reeeling, riting old hippy hopes of a new anti authority
anxiiiious hoping to find a way to keep on living, laughing, leading us all into poetry
prole ole leaves and tatters

C.J. Graham

from one drama queen/to another

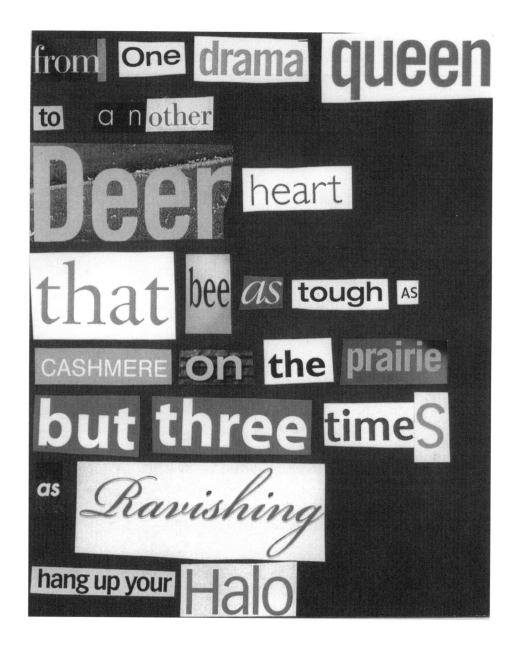

th most xcellent picknik

dew yu remembr that summr day
so long ago out in whiterock
th hill wuz so steep n slippree
th six uv us wur neerly tumbuling
down th green slope uv th grass it felt like we wer rolling
all th way tord th oshun like we wur going 2 maybee
fall
in2 th see

all th brillyant foodz spred out
on th payzlee blankit boild eggz
playts uv anchoveez cheesuz with blew veins
n breds so full uv graynz it seemd
they cud uv maybee falln
floated down like tinee seedz
frum wun uv th treez in th yard

that aftrnoon th sun wuz glowing
like a pinweel in the sky turning
n turning its radyant splendr
on our bodeez evreewher like it wuz
sum kind uv trip we wer all spinning
n laffing about sumthing i cant evun re
member enny more

all uv us totallee filld up
with happeeness n 2 much food
espeshully 4 so erlee in th day
all I know for sher is
we wer in love with th world
so cumpleetlee ekstatik
probablee out uv controll

his lesbian mamas

we would have wanted to
stare at him enraptured
one second, one minute, one hour old
count his miniature toes
touch his tiny button nose
tell him stories of artificial insemination
by zatrian papas
sing lullabies

we would have wanted to
sit side his bed at night
watch for breath
hear his first word
(lightning, do you suppose?)
cheer his first steps
bronze his baby shoes
pack lemon chicken for kindergarten

we would have wanted to
squire him to ballet
watch him skip
assure other boys didn't bully
sit the teachers down for a talking to
sit him down for a talking to
stay away from girls, we might have said
and stairs that go bump in the night

we would have given him
a feather quill
a badger brush
showed him pots of magic green things
at the ends of rainbows

we would have wanted to
settle underneath his head like pillows
and above him like umbrellas

we who love our gay son
without mercy

the bed under the hospital

you have to remember what it was like back then
it was the end of everything, all our dreams, hopes for
a better society, visions of freedom   all gone

we had lost touch,   i can't remember if michael was dead yet
all i know is   bill was up north in recovery from his accident when i wrote
to tell him michael had died, and i was alone with saphira

some big art honcho was having a party at his half-renovated house
and bill leaning against an unsecured door fell straight to the basement
i guess no one told the medics or the emergency staff that he had fallen
because they took one look at his dilated pupils and still strapped to
the gurney he was placed in hallway ready for transfer to crease clinic
and   shock treatment which was being suggested, but bill's guardian
in the form of a woman brain specialist   saw him in the hall and
determined that his was a head injury   and should be operated
like right away,   you have to remember what it was like back then

people used to spit on you and call you names   if they thought you
were a hippie, worse if you were a hippie chick, you were supposed
to give free sex   and get treated like a whore, we were treated like
the homeless because essentially we were, zen buddhist ragged
   vagabonds on the road of life, we had to be there was no money in art
and no community to support it   long ago we chose to throw
   caution to the wind and to make our living in the alternative,
create the flux, the perfect resonating society. how did we go so wrong/

the way the canada council poisoned the community,
with the haves   and the have nots,   creating a hierarchy of power
   governing   the arts   playing politics with peoples souls   and
the dealers   grew strong and rich,   they could afford places to live
fancy cars and women,   adhering to a life of meditation and zen
undermined by a pre-yuppie tidal wave of materialism and bad drugs
shit happens   because the troublemakers   really do exist
like those nurses at the hospital who herded us hippies like animals
brought out the rules and regulations or hysterically accused us of
smoking pot right there in the hospital not allowing us to see our friends
who were sick or injured

it doesn't matter whether i was under bills hospital bed or not
i can't remember a lot about that whole period   as it is
   there was so much misery,   it's something i would have done
to hide from the nurses,   but the idea that he believes
i was there under the bed after his surgery   sending him healing energy,
that is what is im/ portant   it will remain   though   a mystery

Fer bill whoom i luv

frrst tym i met **B**ill i sez to myself, I sez mitch
wow i sez this w**O**n reely shook my chakras up, a
shayk uv miracas kind of saykre**D** chant fr th ages more lyk way beyond the blu
hiz floppy hat doin wut thay **D**o big disnee eyes muv round th room, meat
fyrdup mind **H**ip wit as if th kosmos wuz
s**I**tting off centre
an th **S**tarz bloo owt uv our
eerz in trooth **A**n beeuty i wuznt prepaird i
thot who iz **T**hys messengr frm way up
nor**T**h n how cn we all
b n th saym mu**V**ee with him butt hee sed yoo
Alreddy are !!!

Pauline Holdstock

Considering bill

For I will consider our friend bill

For he is a servant of excellence about the world

For first he is quick to perceive it in the bright day and in the rain and
in the voices of the people

For second he is deft to catch it swift as it be

For third he hath no wish to hoard it

For fourth he labours to increase it

For fifth to dispense it

For sixth he hath faith that there is always more to come

And there always is

For seventh he is thus a teacher of excellence

For eighth he is a student still

For ninth he believes not that excellence has any beginning

Or end

For tenth he sets it down nimbly and exactly

For he is liberal in praise of all parts of the yello day

For his hearing is sharp and can detect even *delicate murmurings of astral journees*

For he wishes for *blessings on all our varied n diffrent business*

For he is the only person who is really like you and like me and how does he do that

For he can see our souls shining through our ordinary clothes

For we can see *th stars n th hope* in his excellent heart

A Prayer for Our Sons

WHAM!
and the boys are back
hungry and transgressive
with their graffiti and dreams

mr. max n mr. spencer! most xcellent! says bill
hey bill they say because
they know cool and bill is cool

they pour in rooms
keeping their boots on
filling space
until the creaking windows bulge
walls crack and burst
with the power of all their cranked up joy,
their fierce, terrifying love.

They straddle borders
between centuries
now and soon
between my body and yours
brothers and friends

and their song will be the tearing up of passports;
they will dance with lightning in their hands
on magic rainbows, fearless, ecstatic

their story will be the story of
the end of all boundaries.

Let them teach us
everything is permitted,
remind us how to break the rules,
let them bless us with their riot,
let them make us look like fools.

Ellen S. Jaffe

I Take Your Poems With Me

whenever I travel
read them like talismans
in strange rooms in Toronto
stars shine on the ceiling

make more sense than theories.

channelling bill

converging over the epicentre of our uncertainty, the weather
is deciding whether or not we will be wet and wanting for more ummm
brellas are everywear when you don't need them and here
in a convertible highway cruiser driven by a man of recent
greeting perhaps the mania is episodal and will pass I would
entertain the redefinition of convertibility at any other time
when the water vapour isn't doing frontal lifts to a height of
39,000 feet that's 12,000 meters or 108 point three repeating
football fields of precipitation and all I did was ask politely
if I could use his bumbershoot and maybe he took it the wrong way
your umbrella I assure him and he says who do you think you are
Mary Poppins?   closer to a morose Fred Astaire   don't worry
we'll get there soon he says   but there's no saying if he means
soon in geological terms and the council of the skies has decided
by unanimous vote booming from the Cariboo to the Kootenays
…I have never been so glad to be wearing running shoes

in the downpour, in the burst sea of Gibraltar, debating
the measurement of running water hatching glop plop
hole in the floorboards plots to bail but he says plug on
before the miraculous appearance of an oasis of convenience
washing the wind off the screen but saving the bugs for me
Fritz knits gnats into transparent infiniteee zeroing in on my lap
waves a motor-hotel-cold-rinse-cycle-laundry-and-home-furnishings hello
flaunting pump a swaying native princess from the Island of Gas
the showering rainbows are out and everyone is drenched in colour
some two or even three tones, others on the back of pick-ups
splattered like Jackson Pollock paintings and the rainbows
come in seven great tastes and people licking and sucking
on anyone wearing their favourite flavour couldn't believe
my luck the day starting out with a heavy storm warning
arctic front moving in behind a ridge of high pressure

maybe he said a bridge of sky pleasure there's no saying
when the weather man might get bored and turn pro
breathing a sky of relief we take off with the evaporating earth
writing raspberry notes on green sun apocalyptic lawn chairs
squeegie parades and retractable feathers and it is all a garden again
just as it was before the dinosaurs learned about meteors and god
would tell us stories to scare us to bed it's no safer inside but drier and warmer
at night sometimes the remote planets of human behaviour come out
some friends who glitter on the pillow taking time for sensible tea
and reasonable mind your pees and queues please leaking information
about the water, about the lack of fish, pollution, price of, theft by US
rain subsidies, rain cheques, the rain loan and savings bank mentality
the evaporating gene pool, expatriating mitochondria, vanishing plankton
and we realize with stuttering sanity that the real problem is sanitation
the western toilet remote control still flushing and promising flowers
the problem is global of course and at the next few drops of rain
we go inside and Noah says he's bringing the inflatable loveseat over
just in case

bill bissett, a photo-portrait

he's on stage, rattle in hand, hat with bandana, feather, loose shirt, chanting, foot keeping rhythm, sounding off to listeners, chanting, building art, a bridge to life, listen to the sound, a journey that begins on the cusp of Scorpio with Sagittarius and Gemini rising – i see him in my camera frame, a shutter-flick moment, later, we walk the ice-cold Montreal streets, he lends me his jacket, talks of his-story, bissett, a trade-name originally brought to Scotland and England from Normandy, ancestors, skilled in the art of placing arrow-tips, martial artists, trace-able to 1198 AD, his forebears once witnessed the charters of William the Lion-Hearted, since then, the clan tartan lost to rivalries, but the meanings and traces remain, bissett, Old French for rock-dove, a gentle bird, grey, flight the colour of stone, a word, stone is stone, but, hear Gertrude's whisper, a stone by any other name, is a rock or Stein, or stan, and then, his Sonic Horses flew high over rock, after the Mandan Massacre, later, music with his Luddites in southwestern Ontario, far from the Norman coastline, and always, drawing the words, painting the world's worth and that beyond. at times along with bp, Birney, & others, creating concrete worlds, selectric, rapid-fire, typewriter visions, paper flights, free spirit, metaphysical rebel-angel, denounced once in the House of Commons for crossing borders others feared to tread, awarmplacetoshit, talking about what we all need, not just physical, but meta-physical, and too close politically to uncomfortable truths, sacred cows, things we all know but no one speaks of, embattled, but defended by no less than Laurence, Atwood, Salinger, and so many others. later, his ride with the Mounties, more than musical, and not-quite-nude descending a staircase, head injury, tucked aside, away, touch-and-go, near death, but a lucky break through a thoughtful nurse, recalled, when he was halfway up the tunnel, revving on the gold light, and music of the soul, suddenly pulled back to the Emergency Ward, iridescent and transcendental, his friends visiting at the hospital, the spirit ship passing totems and mountains, this flight, past control, beyond possession, (it's all done with the mind), in living colour, re-vivifying him with his own poetic energy, sharing what was, is paradise, hopefully, or at least re-sounding, restoring life, the live voice, a blewointment revival, "shamanic," said Kerouac, thinking him native, this son (re-)generates rainbows, let me count the colours: sonic live performer, poem-maker, collage-shaper, calligrapher, typographer, singer-musician, type-writer, publisher, spinning offset, mimeo, xerox, voice, chant, sound-poetry, pulsing in sync with the heartbeat of the sky, painter of incidents on lunaria and other scapes, border-blurs of spirit, mind, body, a post-Blakean internationalist, he always said "nobody owns the earth," not a taker, instead, granting, bestowing, presenting, mystic, anti-commercial, hot political, iconoclastic, counter-culture, mantric, word-scapes, optophonetic maybe, dancing spirit fermenting words/worlds from the unities of sounds drawn by heart from the God-Awful Streets of Man, streams from the psychic flux singing the endless soul that lasts so much longer than we who are just passing through, he, coming joy, dismantling bombs, seizing the means of production, rejecting slavery, reminding us of what we had, have, or could have, and what we do have is poetry, for communication, art, the bridge, and bill singing on stage, the camera eye, one split-second, there's bill in living colour, in the aperture, uncontained, performing, a conduit to ancestral voices & the cosmic flux of all

Adeena Karasick

My Own Private Poet Laureate

I

Recently, i was suffering from a mild case of stage fright.
and this is what bill sd to me: darling, nothing exists except the letters, the words the fiery spaces. feel the letters like sparks flying off the page into your chest through your mouth. one word at a time. feel the weight of them their release into you like magical verbal constructs. like fiery angels blessing you; one word breathing into the next, like dancing stars, clusters, galaxies just keep reading. as each syllable slides into the other & yr breath yr body merging with the letters
because that's all there is,
is those letters, these words, this language

II

If language is a manifestation of structures of the unconscious
If the unconscious is structured by language
If our entry into language emerges at the precise moment that we understand that our subjectivity is split; incessantly spiralling, recombinant (*& as such, is always out of reach*),
for me, this is the infinitely divisible place bill's writing erupts out of –
an aching tumult of fragmented possibilities.

Each letter, a subject, a galaxy (or gala axis) of lexical excess which not only relentlessly pursues ever-elusive objects of desire, but
becomes an intrasubjective matrix of differential relations
displacing all sites of discrimination and domination.

becomes an "incalculable object" projected through "blayzing mysteries," "kaskading perplexities" / and "slushes unberabulee" through the "mirakul" of slow cookin' carrots, "unknowing hungrs," "knawing posisyuns,"
mr n ms understanding.

And though "i lookd for yu in th most dangrous places,"

i am here after 20 years of wading through bissett's
shifting scars, *unravelling* in the suddn spurts where words explode like
(mountains uv creem) burst forth as a textual nexus of dissembling,
desire / masques, perversions, "sparks in the dark"
threading scenarios, lunarias (arias of lunacy) witnessing
through an eye that is pus filled
with throbbed mourning,
with violent ecstasy. And through a series
of ambiguous veils, volés, volleys, voilás. With a
mad frailty, haunted with apparitions (*sans partitions*)
an imprecise visibility which
shudders with
blurred promises
And through this burdened vision, this double vision, he dislocates hierarchic divisions, discursive
transparencies technomediatic fetishizations (fashions, fissions, scissions, collisions), creates for me,
a rapturous palace "kastl" marked by "row[s] uv letters rows uv beautiful letters with the pickshurs
inside them "nite lyric charmrs" where "the narrative line inhabited by raging kreetshurs." And he is
"building houses uv abandond shells," with "tapestreed lobees," "transitive verb konstructs"

And this is the blueprint. an architecture, an aching texture of insignias, that
i now live in – this languescape of syncretistic intersections, hybridized resistences. where each time
approached IS always just out of reach and
"whether konversaysonal vois meditativ rhetorikul image building briks masonree word okal oral
vocal objects puzzul pome opaque n or direct sound,"

i call out
beckoning, madly, desirously painfully
in this excessive *rapport*
(which reports, imports / carries and supports)
& continue to live inside
an endless spiralling of subject positions, circulations of contingent tensions, specifications, locali-
ties, territories, articulations of difference – live
with him inside this
grammar of "unmapabul places," of all that is "trembuling", luxurious and "xcrushiating"
ragingly, magically
split.

Marijke Friesen

the bill bissett card (th fuul)

In the Tarot of the Canadian Poets, the bill bissett card
is th fuul, which can be pronounced as 'the fool' or 'the fuel';
both are bill. It's a logical card for such an entertaining, raging,
playful – and at times – comic poet, but there is more
to th fuul than meets the eye. The wisdom of the ages exists
in his playful mix of words and art.

Th fuul is the 0 card, the mysterious symbol of nothing
and everything, the hole and the circle. A double interlocking zero
on its side, becomes eternity. Everything multiplied
by the zero becomes zero
and everything
divided into the zero becomes the zero. The zero is the place
where the mystical intersects the practical,
the fulcrum point where the negative turns positive
and back again, where the chaotic becomes
subdued and sedated.

The seemingly comic figure of the Fool
or in Native Mythology – the Trickster – is in fact
one of the most powerful cards in the deck.
It is the Hush or 'Shhh' sound in our own language
the connector between Wisdom and its wish to become
manifested in the world with Mercy and Mildness
and that is bill, the fool and the fuel
that connects us all.

A Certain Chance Chant

Wh!
won
One

once
one sin
one sin a

blue
bloom
bloomin'

blue moonin'
blue moon in June

bull
bull loon
balloonin'

sell
sell a bray
celebrate

bill
bill biss
bill bissett

bloom… oooo n

bloom oooo n

Bloo oint meant

Ounce
Once Ha!
Once half
Once having
Once having no
Once having no-one
Once having known you
Once having known youth
Once having known you the
Once having known you the sir
Once having known you the sir ten
Once having known you the sir ten tea
Once having known you the certainty
Once having known you the certainty off
Once having known you the certainty of see
Once having known you the certainty of scene
Once having known you the certainty of seeing you

Once having known you the certainty of seeing you move
Once having known you the certainty of seeing you move all
Once having known you the certainty of seeing you move always
Once having known you the certainty of seeing you move all ways
Once having known you the certainty of seeing you move always moo
Once having known you the certainty of seeing you move always move
Once having known you the certainty of seeing you move always moves me

Once having known you the certainty of seeing you move always moves me stir
Once having known you the certainty of seeing you move always moves me sir then
Once having known you the certainty of seeing you move always moves me sir then
Once having known you the certainty of seeing you move always moves me certainly

Once having known you the certainty of seeing you move always moves me certainly

Once having heard you the certainty of hearing you chant always

chance

certainty

Beth Kinar

ecliptik

see fog rolld in thick
     th nite
         wee billee
bissett
       came in2 this world
   2 paint pomes

    n rage   in flew ent
        raven

    2 grasp all
  uv nothing
     2 grasp

    2 fall thru
  a door
    that lookd like
      a wall

    cum out th othr
side
   n know mor uv us
      than we know
    uv r
      selves

billness

out of yr mouth in every direction
dropped into the well of silence
you nail me down with words

Patrick Lane

FOR bill, FROM patrix

The first time we met we lay on your bed
And read Li'l Abner in the funny papers.
Life was serious back then. It still is,
Though the Sixties seem a century ago,
Fourth Avenue, Blew Ointment, Very Stone House,
Ooljah and Martina, strange days
And stranger nights. Sometimes I can remember
Almost all of it, you and me trudging over
To Pat Lowther's house to talk poetry
And Roy, her murderer, angry because he knew
We thought her wonderful, driving down
To Seattle and the border guards stopping us
On the way home, you breathing through
One nostril, saying you thought it would help,
As they tore the car apart in search of drugs.
Old days, I guess. Mostly I remember
How beautiful you were, how far your dream
Travelled then, how rare your visions. And
How nothing changes, frogs still raining
From the sky over Salmo, perfect green angles
Of transformation, happy at last with a life
They understood. If there is a love in the world
Then you have made of it a poem worth all
The poems I know. How beautiful you were,
How beautiful you are, Li'l Abner still somewhere
Talking to Hairless Joe, Daisy Mae forever
In his arms, and Joe Btfsplk walking alone,
In your eyes without a cloud in the sky.

Four for bill

1. sound gallery

to stand within the sound
gallery still in th red desert
in th green wind that blows
everywhere my mother warned against
th singing bones within those canyons since words themselves
grew whorls of antlers bill
could never be pinned down in
the colours of those particular
reindeer streaming out of cache creek
on a winter day

he's not really a haiku kinda guy
industrial roads notwithstanding
mountainmountainmountain
maybe on th Hope–Princeton goat
gotcha tung gotcha tung
not really a haiku kinda
character caring carrot

rattle voice seed gourd
in a salmon chanted even
shaman chanted evening
with electric green forest
of sound some would yell out
warnings th beach's surf so high
nd poundin don't go there mer
women keening on th shingled beaches storm
is cummin in storm's a cummin in

following th sound
in th nite
in th deth lodj
happily devoted
shaking to be sung
in th stone soup
in th rough stump beating
th hollow gourd
with th rivers in it
yr axe man
following
th sound
of th waves
on th beach of sun
no end no beginning
in th foamin of th dancers
on th moonlit sand

2. coastal love

how rapidly can yu take dictation.
Driving faster than yr headlights
Not good for most of us most of the time

Silence and rage merge
In the roar of Pacific breakers
At Pachena, Florencia, and Schooner

The trees shakjin their green rattles
Th gulls dancing th two-step in th surf

Do they speak to us tonight
Can we carry their songs forward
To th thirsty stones
Lay a bridge on interstellar space

Lookup we're home
Writing lovers
In flaming script
Text that collapses
on a raga page

there is no news
that bill would not
perfect, bill
legally tender
duck's brilliant & horny
yellow hand, trumpet, sieve.

Many birds pass thru these spaces,
Between th fingers
Of these hands

Rapidly
As in acid strobe
Empty out
Into th lite.

3. for th midisin bag, a gift

    thinkin about a chinees pome
    kwatrain fused empteebreth
      yet staind with plum
    & in leather shakin, th sun
    rockin off th rim

4. th 60s on 4th

present yet apart
from th other side of th countree
so many footsteps of hiway
to live on rooftops
by kitsilano bay

I ching incense ooljah goofing
& mike on speed or mushroom
th tea is always dragons
sipped thru lightning doorways,
tansy still blooming on down 4th

we were practicing up
to be human, as lionel sd,
on salmon chanted evenings,
a tiny tribe
that felt so huge, who
new

d.a.levy

PART **2**

The Bowl in the Bodhisattva's Hand

to

Lokeshvara.

th. The ... their fabric is ...

Carol Malyon

illuminaysyun

the dream of enlightenment a candle
flickering in the dark cave of the mind
until we holler *i see! at last i see!* or
eureka! like archimedes

the need for a wise old woman ancient crone
sage or medicine man who learned the old
stories & is able to pass them on tongue
speaking an antique language eyes that have
seen everything   a scarring on the brow
third eye-eye remnant   glowing gemstone
at the throat   we would stare   be hypnotized
but are already tranced by the eyes

to be chanting in a sweat house   dancing
the heart slowing   slipping into synchronicity
with the great pulse of the earth   a fetus
rocking in a salt sea   the mother's heartbeat
throbbing all around it   adrift in that soothing
rhythm   separate   apart   but never alone

a face appearing in the forest   indistinct
through the trees   my companions see nothing
try to pull me away   but are unable   rootlets
unfasten from my feet to grab the earth   light
shimmers   each living thing separates from
its companions   each leaf cleaves from other
leaves   becomes distinct   individual   luminous

i need to experience this too   don't hold
my hand love   this magic can only happen
when we stand   kneel fall down   alone

False Portrait of bill bissett as William Wordsworth
After William Hazlitt

His mind is obtuse, except
when it is the organ and receptacle
of accumulated feeling

a linnet's nest startles him
the tall rock lifts its head
in the erectness of his spirit
and the lamb looks up to him
with sparkling eye.

Nursed amidst the grandeur of Vancouver's
mountain scenery
he has turned back partly
from the bias of his mind
and sought out the Muse among sheep-cotes
and hamlets, hinds and shepherds.

He condemns all French writers in the lump
the Ode and Epode, Strophe and Antistrophe
he laughs to scorn. No sad

vicissitude of fate deforms his page
as he gathers manna in the wilderness
and elevates the mean on fluttering wings.

Mr. Bissett in his person
is above the middle size with
marked features, and an air somewhat stately if quixotic
his manner of reading his own poetry is
particularly imposing with chants and rattles
that turn apple dumplings into heartfelt sentiments.

Though his style is vernacular
and delivers household truths
the swellings of his language resemble
heavenly symphonies
or the healing power
of plants or herbs.
His sonnets, indeed, have something
of the same high-raised tone and prophetic spirit
and if his poems were read aloud in Elysium
the spirits of departed heroes and sages
would gather round to listen in!

Mr. Bissett is often silent, indolent and reserved
if he has become verbose and oracular
in late years, he was not so in his better days.
(He did not court popularity by a conformity
to established models, and he ought not to have been
surprised that his originality was
not understood as a matter of course.)

Yet the tide has turned much in his favour
in late years he has met the Queen, has
a large body of determined partisans
and is at present sufficiently
in request with the public
to save or relieve him from
the last necessity to which a man of genius
can be reduced –
that of becoming the daffodil
of his own idolatry!

Xcellent Birds

half our clothes off
bill, Helen, and i follow Ronn
under Enderby Bridge
into Shuswap River

bill says he and i are
easygoing gradualists
because of the way
we approach the river

we have become river gods
and goddesses, now transformed
by river smell and penetrating sun
that drives us into cool water

bill and i swim to an island
where everything is different
a wolf print lingers among wild
strawberry plants

when we leave the river
soggy clothes heavy with sand
we come across four silent
grounded birds

they stand poised on a cliff
while we cluck and coo over them
wondering our human questions
but these silent birds are a mystery

they may be doves, i say
there are 4 of us and 4 doves, offers Helen
doves are love, says Ronn
xcellent beautiful xcellent, says bill

we all agree but later when i search
my bird books, unable to identify them,
i'm mystified maybe it was a group
hallucination, says bill, or maybe

it was the way we approached the river.

Susan McMaster

2 charmin billee

billy bloo balloo
grayt hulla-baboo
in stant roarz
stanz abuv us
all thru yr rool-zapt rood
yr chantz n rippin toonz
yu sussed us well
bling-blang ring-rang
westrlee pub man
publish rub man
lush man fish man
scroo-ee boom man
wingd yr way
in 2 r eerz
in 2 r wordz
we herd yu cleer
miztr bloo
danst n pranst
2 yr wing-a-ding-tool
uv noyz n nooz
uv rowzin eye-deez
rippin yr rukus
rokin throo us
it wuz yu bill uv kors
so manee wayz yu
4 wher uv yu bin
billee boyo
tell us troo
hear ther n evree dam wher
showtin owt my growl
beebeebuzzn
sownd rezowndn
in spr ay shun 4 us all
thnx then n now n next
sind bill-struck
sooo

I welcome back the magic boy

with the gentle voice
  humming memories
your fire has been lighting
  othr horizons
my flame has been gentle
  and quiet
my words have been sticking
to the roof of my mouth
because the doors
        though open
            have been holding a darker sign
I welcome back the magic boy
  with the playful mouth
      sighing "beautiful"
even when you were standing close
  and I muttered bullshit
I needed your sigh
    to wash through me
I haven't felt as innocent
  since your crazy eyes
  stopped dancing around my poetry
I welcome back the magic boy
  who let me wear my words
in a bright flag across my heart
  I tried to draw on memory
tried to read your crazy clothes
  to imagine your crazy shoes
        rocking your chair on two legs
to hear your laughter in quiet gulps
  sporadically musicing the evening

I got a little lost
   without the boy
and maybe I did start bashing something
   but without your prolific music
to set my dreams to
      I hid
I welcome back the magic boy
     with the gentle voice
and though I've found my own
    I will never forget
the night
      my poetry danced…

A Dream Poem About bill bissett Cooking

he was Elvis first
I peered through a small window
to watch him peeling onions
his double was there too
they moved together quietly
around the kitchen
without speaking
totally concentrating on cooking

cooking is all there is

then he was bill bissett
still cooking
I was inspired to write a poem
it began with eggs cracking

cracking eggs   opening the shell
the liquid oozes into the bowl
throwing away the shells
beating the yolk into the white
mixing   mixing
peeling onions   chopping them into
small bits
sautéeing them in a pan
sizzling garlic
smells   pungent and nose-tingling
mouth-watering
vegetables of all kinds

phallic carrots   the oh so womanly
artichoke hearts
greenness of peas and beans
peppers   red and yellow
spots of colour
dancing in the pan

but this is only a shadow
of the dream poem
the ur-poem
the one that captured so perfectly
the fluid movements of bill
of Elvis   and his double
gliding like dancers   slowly and softly
as I watched through
a small window
their silent
cosmic   spiralling

from No. 9 of *the small blue*

i am thinking
of the early poems
of bill bissett

how there can be
empathy in a voice
that simply says so

and geography
as people inhabit
with words

leaves change and autumn
acorns scatter across the
drive looking for the earth

i understand them
in some far off
invented way

there's a white
trimmed sky against
the planet

the reflection
a season has
before it's too late

Gustave Morin

somebody owns the earth

there/s money in the shark...there/s shark in the money...there/s money in the shark...there/s shark in the money...there/s money in the shark...there/s shark in the money...there/s money in the shark...there/s money in the shark...there/s shark in the money...there/s money in the shark...there/s shark in the money...

(concrete poem composed of the repeated phrases "there/s money in the shark...there/s shark in the money..." arranged to form an image)

Somewhere Under the Rainbow

I meet you in the lobby of the Hotel Macdonald.
They've decorated for Thanksgiving
with hay bales and pumpkins.
At first, I think you're part of the decor:
the scarecrow from the Wizard of Oz.
You're wearing 6 jackets,
and your hair looks like straw.
You tell me, "Somewhere
there's a yellow brick road,"
and suggest we find it.
"No chance," I say.
"This is Edmonton.
It's 21 below."

I want to buy you lunch,
you want to go to the bus station.

We walk one frozen block
to the Sunterra.
I buy you a bowl of some green soup,
then you decide it's time to go.
We find a taxi that won't take you as a fare.
"He'll freeze!" I shout.

Oh, Mr. b, you've got dreams of Canmore
and I'm courting death in downtown Edmonton.
I give you a big so-long kiss
and suddenly the icy street
turns into clattering, sunny yellow bricks.

Susan Musgrave

"We Come This Way But Once"
A poetry reading tour of England, Wales, Scotland and Paris with bill bissett and George Johnston October 25–November 9, 1980

I

I don't know how they keep
this train on the tracks
the wheels turn and that's it
in two weeks
bill will be chopping wood
in the Cariboo, I'll be
down in Panama and George
back with his family.

I don't know how they keep
this train on the tracks
with all the distractions
they have to face daily.

I've been faithful to Paul
for nearly six weeks
it's not exactly easy
in fact it's a record.

I don't like sleeping alone
at night I like to hold someone.
When I start to dream about
old relationships, then it is
especially difficult.

bill says you have to wait
two years in between
major relationships
I've been waiting a few weeks
and already I'm impatient.
I don't know how they keep
this train on the tracks,

the wheels turn and
that's it.

The men along the line are
smoking, talking
bill says "in two hours
I can smoke." I don't know
how he does it.

I don't know how anyone does,
I just want to hold someone and
right now it's not possible
it never is when you
really want to   there is no one
there is really no one.

The wheels turn and
that's it   the train
stays upright, it's designed
like this.

The men along the line
are hunched against the cold
I watch them   they watch me
George says the cold is
piercing.

Yesterday at church I got
a message on my palm;
bill saw it and touched it.
bill got a message, too;
Mrs. Peel, the healer, saw
a question in his life.

In Vancouver one time I saw
a question mark on the mountain.
I was upstairs holding some
TV personality, my life
was on the line, I changed,
that was it

there clearly was, that day,
a question mark on the mountain,
and now on my palm, and in
bill's life.

But last night when we talked
I wrapped myself in his words
and there I wasn't cold anymore
I wasn't scared or lonely.

Later I had a dream – we moved to
Arizona. bill and I could actually
go there; George, of course, could
bring his large good family.

    II

In yellow Wellingtons I went
to Sylvia Plath's grave
on a cold day in November –
bill was with me.

We'd heard she was buried in
unconsecrated ground
it's all the same now, the vicar
told us   he hadn't known her
personally.

At first we couldn't find her –
the cold was making it hard.
Maybe she did it to get warm
bill said. That must have been part of it.

I found a blue suitcase
in among the weeds –
someone had lost it or
left it behind, no doubt
a worn-out traveller. I too
would like to get rid of some
weight. I carry so much with me
and most of it unnecessary.

The grave was wild, I guess
that's good. I would not choose
a tidy grave myself – nor any grave:
the day will come when I have
no choice.

It's all the same now
standing at the grave's edge
bill with the blue suitcase
packed and matching the
blue shoes he'd worn out
with so much travelling.

We sat for hours in a pub
away from the cold and talked
of unrelated things. By that
I mean we avoided love or grief.

And high above Heptonstall
a cold moon hung in the sky,
a blond thing with a yellow rose
on its side   a funny duchess
a suicide.

III

The time I like best is
when we are alone and talking

this isn't a romance
so it's all right to laugh

I don't think I laughed once
all summer in Mexico
I didn't talk much either.
Lovers are quite serious, you say.
I agree, it's curious.

And complicated sometimes.
One woman you knew had herself
sterilized   I wonder
if that simplified anything
or simply hurt

we hide our hurt well
but this isn't a romance.

If it were a romance
and you brushed against me
the way you do now, in
friendship, it would probably
mean something. If I
waited for you to call and
you didn't, it would probably
hurt and I wouldn't hide it.

This isn't a romance.

Not laughing gets serious
sometimes   for instance
when you are leaving someone
or they are leaving

I mean people are always
leaving   next week
so will You

but it's all right to laugh
it's all right to laugh.

IV

The silver bracelet
bill didn't get
is still in the window

I dreamed of it again last night
I had wanted to buy it for
him and he for someone else
but isn't that always how it is
I mean   as long as you live
your case is very doubtful.

You decide, say, not to live.
You think you are dying to
punish someone when really
you are dying to free them

that's a good enough reason
for staying alive

and all this over one
silver bracelet.

The bracelet was in the window
of a shop owned by Mr. Benson.
His neighbour told us he was
never open. They no longer speak:
Mr. Benson, she said, is a bit
of a twister.

We might find him at the library
where he goes to read the news.
"A single sentence will suffice
for modern man: he fornicated
and he read the papers."

That's our Mr. Benson. Hot on
his trail we hightailed it
down to the library. He was late,
it wasn't like him, said the
librarian. He wore a beard and a
black cloak – his grandfather
was a warlock.

bill searched every café (George
took the 9:06 up to Newcastle)
I thought perhaps Mr. Benson
was in bed, having overslept
or died – the ultimate sentence.

But we found him walking back
to open the shop   he never
opened before noon he said,
but for the silver bracelet
one hundred and fifty pounds

sterling! bill was prepared to
pay around thirty   I would have
gone higher and given it to him
so that he, in turn, could
give it as a gift

but things don't actually work
like this – my case would still
have been doubtful.

The silver bracelet
bill didn't get
will always be in that window

on it a young girl and a
man who is also unattainable.

They do not touch though their
fates are intertwined.   Together
they shine   in bill's eye,
in mine.

V

"I heard some good news today,"
said George. "We come this way
but once." We were on a train
between London and Brighton –
I seem to remember having
come this way before.

It was ten years ago and the
circumstances were similar.
I was waiting to meet a man
on whom all my life depended.
He was late, I recall, or else he
never arrived. Years later I can't say
it makes any difference.

I am still waiting, there is
still no one. In the station at
Brighton I heard George Harrison sing
"I really want to see you but it
takes so long…"

Last night in Oxford I dreamed
I went blind. I was high up in the
sky, as usual I was waiting for
someone. Whoever it was arrived
but then I couldn't see him.
bill dreamed our ship was about to
go down. George dreamed, blissfully,
nothing.

In my life my dreams are the
only continuity   bill the same
though I can't speak for him.

I suspect as much   when the ship
sank he stayed with it. I, too,
though floundering. Others, around
us, abandoned the ship and drowned.

VI

The terrible parting in
Paris or London has yet
to come, with all the sadness
rolled into one

but you can't hedge on the wheel.

Today we're together in
Glasgow. It's starting to feel
permanent; all the hotels,
the lonely stations, they're
starting to feel familiar.

In Norwich I saw a church
that had been bombed by a
Zeppelin and in Coventry the
new cathedral. By Cardiff
we were thoroughly festive.

bill was kept awake in Dundee
with the election on television
and a toilet endlessly flushing

I slept through dreams of
one train pulling away after
another
we were saying goodbye
on a platform in some station
it meant we would
stop travelling together
it meant we would go on alone
and in different directions.

George had gingercake and honey
I had a handful of rain
I said what use to anyone
is a handful of rain
I am always trying
to make sense out of things.

I want everything to last,
at least to stay the same.
bill says I should let it all go
you can't hedge on the wheel.

So I turn and the wheel
turns and the sadness turns too
into tears and laughter, the
unspeakable circuit

one train pulls away after
another and all the sadness
is rolled into one.

What use is a handful of
rain I say   away with it!
Let it go!

Bill Bissett Let Himself Into My Room

and shook me awake. It was only about noon so I was still asleep. "Brian! Get up! We need pictures!" Bill and his poet-musician cohorts The Mandan Massacre were putting out a record. They dragged me the dozen or so blocks to the roof of Bill's apartment where I shot off a quick half-dozen rolls of 120 film in my $85 Yashica twin-lens reflex camera. No coffee, no food. That's my excuse.

What's yours?

I met Bill (who spells his name fully lower-case, even the *Canadian Encyclopedia* spells it lower-case, but I don't because I'm a rebel) in 1963. He lived with Martina and their newborn girl, Ooljah, in a large street-level apartment that consisted of two enormous rooms at the corner of Yew and York in Vancouver. I went there one late afternoon with Gil Pomeroy and Neri Gadd. The five of us (Ooljah slept) ate a large quantity of peyote, walked the few blocks to the beach and watched the sun.

I sat on a gigantic washed-up tree stump most likely in that same spot still. Then we walked back to the flat. After a while I felt sick and realized I was dying.

Then I died. Then I was born.

I'm not kidding around – that's exactly how it all happened that very night that lasted till dawn broke and I walked home a completely new being. Although with time

I became once again the same being I'd been all along.

Seven years later I was at Bill's with George Heyman. I gave George some poems for his magazine, *Circular Causation*, but said I needed a pen name. Bill said, "use Nation" and that's been my name since. Interesting because seven years earlier I thought of Bill as the paternal figure
of my new birth experience and here he was
giving me my name.

Sharon H. Nelson

dansing magik animals

dissolving critical distance   bill bissett's iconography
dansing magik animals   *hearts n rings*
acrylic on canvas   1991

the paint is thick and golden,
and the *magik animals*
lift their red and blue bodies with joy,
the joy of bodies dancing

that image we share   of getting clear
of what stops the flow of energy that makes
wings of our arms   springs of our legs,
the muscles and the bones   the heart and the mind   lifting
so that we fly towards each other,
no mystical mysteries of levitation or transcendence
but simply bodies dancing

the boundaries of earth air fire water blur;
all those imposed separations,
the categories by which we set boundaries
to keep each other out
disappear in the golden air,
denied by our bodies when we dance,
when we rise to meet each other above the categories,
when we rise to meet each other
trying to be fully human   crying to be fully human
above the din of politics and propaganda that tell us
we are not light or beautiful enough to dance

if we clear our throats, clear a space for song,
for the rhythms we know   in our feet   in our hands
that we can stretch whole bodies towards
if we lift our arms   lift our heads,
elongate our torsos and our necks,
and vault into the golden yellow air
where the *magik animals* are dancing

we discover
a universe of joyous dancers,
each of us capable of rising,
each of us capable of trying
to lift into the golden yellow air
to join the dance the *magik animals* are showing us
trying to be fully human,
stretching above the categories,
reaching towards each other   all of us dancers
regardless of our shapes or our deformities

the war against politics and propaganda
towards clarity and full humanity
has not broken us yet

we become *magik animals*
stretching towards each other,
discovering the possible extensions of our bodies,
how great are the possible extensions of our bodies
when we try to be fully human,
when we rise above the categories,
when we rise, loving, to dance

Sharon H. Nelson

ponee xpress

the tape unwinds and winds
ium lying on the floor   concentrating
breathing   contracting   stretching
trying to relax   muscles   lengthen   the spine
and i think of your body   wondring
how's yr chest   what's the state uv   yr abdominals
whut is happening   to   yr back

the letter carrier   who used to be the mailman
slams envelopes thru the slot   bangs the door   with force
you'd think he hates   to deliver   poems

i rush to the door   gather up the mail
yr bodee still in my hed
now the bodee uv yr text
is in my hands   new poems
and inquiries about my health

what kind of intimacy   are we achieving here?
poets who discuss   lungs   spines   musculature
glands in the brain   you say
i speak of neural networks   everything connected
visceral animals   flexing the muscles in our heads
the seat of intelligence   probably in the gut   as once believed
the seat of love   below the heart   at the centre   of   gravity

2

skies in the north are clear   and keep   no secrets
stars speak   without hesitations   without obscurities
it's easy to hear   if we listen   carefully
if we love   enough   the sound   of bodees   breathing

the sky breathes   continuously   we hear
wind rushing   breathe in   the cold air   it might
catch us   in th throat   or lungs
but we practise   breathing   and writing   poems
in which   celestial   bodies   move   breathing

language   a dance
extension   across
whole continents

peopul ask   how can we hear   the same music?
how do we know   we're keeping   time?
set the poem   on the page
and we breathe it   the same

```
bpNichol
```

a poem by bill bissett

deer in the forest
between   the trees
where i   sense them
    the traces   their hooves leave
        in the wet earth

            wet
        day   i cannot
            remember
        the way   they
        used to   move
            then   when
            i was
                younger

                younger
            days
        the hunger
                returns
            the dry   reds
            the nights   the sky
                burned

                * * * * *
                * * * * *
            * * * * * * *
            * * * * * *
            * * * * *

                    along the highway
            starry
                        night
    the white
                    line
            burns
                        the eyes
            deer
                        crossing
    where the mind
                        moves
        (
            (   )   )
    (   )   )
            (   )
                                        goodnight
            the mountains
                            mass against the sky
        like clouds
                    peaks
                        invisible
        where the deer roam
                            proud and
                wild

given to me in a dream & transcribed
january 17   1967

```
bpNichol
```

Book of Common Prayer (excerpt)

for Bill Bissett

"a funny name for claimd similur creaturs
one a porpoise th othr a dolphin"

saint of no-names
saint of kisses

your lips are on me
sharp-tooth & giggle-eye

final voices in the living room
sick in bed with grief
walked out the door that last time & told you

bled my mouth dry for words

later:

try to write the poem i breathe in

noise
what level of

did you moving back and forth there thru her
yes & handled him the change

all these noises &
screaming

stiff-shouldered in the chair
where's the muse will save me

USELESS SAINTS
YOUR FUCKING LIES &

jesus sweet jesus eyes
skin of blessing
did i catch it in a cup
for saving?

all things fall

all things are one in the end

all that is all encompassed in that word

ah sweet saints of sameness
you are that saint

his all

bissett

It is somehow implicit
that I can't write in "bissett"
and surely illicit.
But I praise it and kiss it
when bill writes in "bissett"

Driving to the Airport

i asked bill
about love

bill said:

i wasn't
going to call him
and i didn't
for 2 months
the whole time
i was here

then
last night
at 2
in the morning
i broke down
and i called

he said:

> *you BELONG to me*
> *you belong to ME,*
> bill

isn't that great?
he said
that i belong to him

and i do
so want
to belong
to someone

between the hours
of one and three
in the morning
if you know
what i mean

ORANGES.
   Build is all right.

Build is all right. Build is all around.
Build is all right. Build is all around.
Build is all right. Build is all around.
Build is all right. Build is all around.
Build is all right. Build is all right.
Build is all right. Build is all round.
Build is all right. Build is all round.
Build is all right. Build is all round.
Build is all right. Build is all round.
Build is all right. Build is all round.
Build is all right. Build is all round.
Build is all right. Build is all round.
Build is all right. Build is all round.
Build is all right. Build is all round.
Build is all right. Build is all round.
Build is all right. Build is all round.
Build is all right. Build is all round.
Build is all right. Build is all round.
Build is all right. Build is all round.
Build is all right. Build is all round.
Build is all right. Build is all round.
Build is all right. Build is all round.
Build is all right. Build is all round.
Build is all right. Build is all round.
Build is all right. Build is all round.
Build is all right. Build is all round.
Build is all right. Build is all round.
Build is all right. Build is all round.
Build is all right. Build is all round.
Build is all right. Build is all round.
Build is all right. Build is all round.
          Build is all round.

4 bill bissett

Sleeping with bill

we sleep inside each other all
                                    –bill bissett

I slept under your paintings last night
in a hotel room overlooking English Bay.
Walls adorned with universes of you:
yellow skies explode in naked throats,
mountains peaks erupt beneath shoulder blades,
watery blue birds coo in your lungs.

I'm awoken at dawn by a restless poem
flapping in the wind, its edge
chopping at the desktop, the corner
of its page held down by the slender
weight of Gertrude Stein's *Tender Buttons*.

The poem, like all poems scattered
throughout this room, is about
you. The boundless wayz u r loved.
These sublime scriptures
each page a love song.

I sit by the window, rest my feet on the ledge,
light a cigarette & capsize a sleepy freighter
under my big toe. A seagull sails by,
turns its head toward me, and is caught
by the swirling energy of this room
fed by wind & the hangover
of last night's dreams. A moment later,
I'm startled by its scraping claws landing on
the concrete ledge, inches from my feet.
He pokes his head under the window,
pecks at the ashtray and vanishes with a butt.

It's not long before I feel the bite
of the bay breeze, and close the windows.
The room slips into an eerie calm,
the waking sounds of the city now muted.
And the poem that had tender wings, folds itself
gently atop Gertrude Stein, as if to shield her
from the morning light.

Let her sleep a little longer.

Jeff Pew

the day bill bissett
blew into town

people appeared like curious crop circles
forgot most earthly conventions
how 2 spel   keep trak uv time   th wet lawndree
still in th dryer

no wun cud xplayn th suddn urge
2 hug eech othr

The day bill bissett
blew out of town
people soberly went back about their business
unpacked dictionaries, set watches
made neat starched creases in their clothes
yet when they looked in mirrors

thay saw brillyant smyles
nevr seen b4

writing thru: "pass th food
release the spirit book" for
bill bissett:

axiiieeeee, passport photo
of the human soul, blank
exspense, feck weed, assist
trance, rites of copy, blank
trance, blank reverse, moshun,
th endless noise, tord,
sumhow, whun ja kuna, speekin
tongues, oh you oh you, a,
the letter exposed, jgingo k
fann, oh you oh you, opn, kokok,
ngnn jandee fakn, sun rising
between hills, profile line,
ja kunnn, ha mnt chuka yuka
ha mna dee, trew, jadact,

a <u>warm</u> p<u>lace</u> t<u>o</u> sh<u>it</u>

viznalizeshun of th word, cum,
this aint no capitalist pome,
togo, dirty concrete poet,
caffin, dot penis, whnnnawhnn
whnnnawhnnnawhnnnawhnnna,
assa, spinnin hand, jakum,
trew trew trew, blend yr
sorrow, what if i go crazy,
bird yu cum to me, yu dont nee
rargins, npsn, march sixth two
thousand and four, we shnd
finish this coffee, yes,
omomomomomomomomomomom,
th need to eliminate
narcotic laws, hand signs,
mandalla, no thunder today,
neom neom neom neom neom,
hawaya, sun rising between
cheeks, dreem, what fukan
thery, oblivion, trewtrewtrew,

Jamie Reid

i went to see bill nd he told me

that his sistr hd gon
ovr to spirit as he calld it
nd she hd cum back to tell him
it was bettr ovr ther than heer

the erth is th worst place she told him
evry othr place is bettr.

Fiona had a seezhur durin the nite
nd was criticul in th hospitul
she's deciding whethr r not to go ovr
to the spirits, bill sd to Wendy nd to Dermot.

this is a vale of tears he sd,
but there's joy heer too,
isn't ther?

later he told me abt his frst muthr,
who died of cancer when he was just a littl kid,
nd about his second muthr, "who went into the oshun,"
luving needls and used to rite to him about it
whn he luvd needls too.

its not fair of God, he sd, to allow pain,
do yu think so, Jamie? its so unnecessary, isn't it?
we reely cd liv without it, cdnt we?

biseteez

biseteez

th most strik
in eksternl
feechur of
bill bissett's
vers is
uv cors
its uneek
ORTHAW
GRAFEE
wch is not

STRIKT
LEESPEE
KING a
difrunt
form uv
orthawgrafee
PURR SAY
but is insted
orthawgrafee

uv anuther
langwage
HEER
to be kalld
biseteez
in realitee
a uneek
ideeolekt

SPESHULL
YADAPTED
t crtn kindz
of meeningz
as frensh is
sd t b th
langwage
uv luv nd
english

uv commurs
th kindz
uv meeningz
wch cannot
b eezilee
kontaynd

bis teaze

in norml
ENGLISH
nun uv all
th yuzhual
kryteereea
uv gud vers
cn b aplied
t ths at frst
STRANGE
langwage

that eezilee
with a litl
efort bcums
COMPLET
LEE
FAMILIUR
KOMPRES
HUN
wch in uthr

POETS
standz in
DIREKT
relashunship
t ther kraft
in biseteez
ths wel
known craft

is jetisond
in favor uv
EGSPANSH
UN like crtn
GASZ
EKSPLODI
NG or watr
BRAYKING
out uv damz

wut we hav
insted uv
KLOSLY
argued and
stated
FEELINGZ

bi st eez

EMOSHUN
Z thots etc
is runaway
LANG
WAGE
langwage
unreestraynd
HENS
LOOS
all ovr th

PLAYS
nd our own
feelingz
az reedrz
follow this
kwite eezily
in biseteez
nd therby
sumtimez

find ways
uv escape
tho if it wer
TRANS
LATD into
NORML
ENGLISH
it probablee

WDNT
make eny
sens at all
biseteez
REKOGNI
ZEZ
nd therbye
overthrows
throws ovur

entire ordrs
uv speech
nd with this
OVER
THROW
INAWEGU

bi st iz

RATES
whol new
relms of thot
nd feeling
yu see thingz
that wer
alweez
ther but yu
cdnt alweez
see thm

being blinded
by th wurdz
r betr yet
made def by
THEM
becuz things
of difrent
ORDRS
ar thrown

TOGETHR
SEEMINGL
EE without
reegard for
norml
katagorees
yu bcum
abl t see

KONEKSH
UNS
previuslee
HIDN
biseteez
by making
wurdz vizibl
reestorz thm
makes yu

see what yu
didnt see
heer
what yu
didnt heer
properlee

b is it is

bfor it
makes yu
blind & def
so that yu
cn see
nd heer
BETR
by destroying
WURDZ
biseteez

leevs room
fr the
RESUREK
SHUN
of langwage
as a meenz
not so much
uv saying
nd uv

MEENING
but uv being
lik dansing
or singing
not knowing
th tune
r th time
making it up

as yu go
ALONG
nd thats what
poetree is for
MAYBEE
biseteez is
UTHER
WORLDLY
sumtimez too

ALTHO
mor often it
letz wurdz
speek fr
themselvz
NAKEDLEE

Randy Resh

MR blissett

Buddha beatific,
ORA-tor-ic rhet-or-if-fic
Howlin' Harlequinne Hierophant:
Tongue-
A-Tone-a
-ma-Tur-gy.

Shaman Synticillant
chanting, in-canting
iridescent, incandescent,
effervescent X-cell-ency!

Follow your bliss:
whispered whim of wisp
aches the rattle,
shakes side saddle
magick carpet,
raging rainbow ride!

Follow your bliss:
whim without a wanting wisp;
allusive, elusive
bliss-fish this.

Follow your bliss:
whatever your wish;
Buddha be-at-ific
ora-Taro-tic rhet-or-if-fic.

The MR blissett bids bliss:
on the chant of a charm-a
karmaclaspkiss.

the lower case lover

He changes his name all the time. We
forget where we found him, but never
mind; he's gone again, his magic green
gum stuck on every surface,
his bed so unmade we might think
he'd shared it with a tree full of
monkeys – all of them dreaming
they were dancers in the time before
movies and doctors who cut people
open to let the pinch fairies out.

The first time he dreamed he was
flying, his father told him boys with wax
wings melt, and, at certain velocities,
the sea turns to concrete. Why do fathers
like that see the ocean half empty?
Are they the ones who make bad
things happen – the Jacks who fall
down the stairs, the Jills who hear voices
and children who sleep in the snow?

It is lower case love at first sight every
starry night in Montreal or London or
New York when the band keeps playing
and he puts himself into the dance
between grief and drowning. He always
turns up when we need him, leaves
again when some other ship's going
down, tells the grieving that snow is only
water waiting to melt and carry on.

He told us he was the water inspector
and said water with an important T.
He came with oranges and felt pens, and
those magic green things that grow
in the sap of trees where monkeys
whistle like the families in Mexican
markets who never lose one another.

Is he a whale now, swimming with radar,
whistling for lost boys? Is he a sheep in
sheep's clothing trying on a song by Bach?

The last time we saw him, he was sitting
in the window, watching Mennonite
television. It had to be movies that
showed him the world was flooding
this time, and the man next door was up
on the roof planting orange seeds in
his gutters so there would always be
orange blossoms and oranges to eat,
even when the man's ladder has been
swept away by the water. He hasn't
flown home for the holidays. He can't
put Christmas in the shopping cart
he wheels from gig to gig, telling his
stories about magic green things
growing on trees so we can glue
ourselves back together and get
everyone up and flying again.

Linguistic Foreplay

"bill bissett is the foremost experimental poet in the country. His lyrics intimidate the linear academic mind. it is has subtleties in cadences and linguistic foreplay leading up to making love to text, or a poem – that is directed to the audiophile more than the poet taster. In short, bill can upset a logophile hung up on plot – narrative and a fetishistic exactness of grammatical and synthetic structures, commonly known in the phrase of "making sense." he is a nightmare for bibliographers, librarians, bureaucrats on the Canada Council and even to some humourless musicologists, and then, let us face, there is the mischievous intent, the comedic trickster in revving psychic steam in his approach to cathartic but live entertainment. too alive for my conservative neuro-system. what in hell do you say when you see a guy ecstatically trying to provoke the rain god, do you say this guy, this man child – why he is a madman, even now after four decades I see this entranced poet tapping his toes and shaking his tambourine and timbers. i think he is vibrating between Id and Super Ego and fear he will take him over the limbic goal line. now the one thing i like about people he has hung in there since the early sixties and hasn't complained about public apathy to poets, has been generous to poets. sometimes he goes too far afield – to the elastic limit – with addressing me as JR: what's new JR. what do you think, JR and then what rattles my septuagenarian timbers the most is one word – the way he says : exxxxxxxxxxxxselent JR eeeeeeeeeeeeeexsellent. bill bissett is a satirist for every age. his poetics defy tight little concepts on linguistics. i am sure Chomsky would not be amused, and then, hearing bill make a poem come alive off the page might just amuse any linguistic supernova of a scholar. bill is a Canadian resource – and his poetry should be taught not by English Dept and certainly not creative writing – but by experimental composers in residence at some elite college – somebody knows a mystic, a born again Blake-sparked poet – a poet of every age, a subversive poet, a mentor to the young, the budding poet with un-tinselled ears – and to those having made their contribution to Lady Muse and now face crepuscular old age. Exxxxxxxxxxxxxxxxxxxsellent bill------exxxxxxxxxxxxxxxxxsellent."

Stuart Ross

A Pantoum for bill

A seagull swooped by, and the rainbow was singing
And a monkey shrieked glee from its perch on bill's wrist
We embraced and we kissed on the post office steps
And the guys who'd yelled Faggot! just looked on in silence

A monkey shrieked glee from its perch on bill's wrist
And on Earth Day it rained as we danced at City Hall
The guys who'd yelled Faggot! just looked on in silence
The chugging of maracas filled the candlelit room

On Earth Day it rained as we danced at City Hall
And bill sliced up oranges, served them with tea
The chugging of maracas filled the candlelit room
The first time I saw bill, Rosenblatt's eyes rolled

Bill sliced up oranges, served them with tea
We lounged in the courtyard and talked about death
The first time I saw bill, Rosenblatt's eyes rolled
Everything's bill-shaped, the trees and the clouds

We lounged in the courtyard and talked about death
We embraced and we kissed on the post office steps
Everything's bill-shaped, the trees and the clouds
A seagull swooped by, and the rainbows were singing

Message from Lunaria
(CosmoSonnet for bill bissett)

if i show you the divots on my kneecap,
will you consider an alien abduction?
            –famous Lunarian poet

the earth looks pretty shattered from here
swaths of brown where forests used to be
what green is left smudged out by haze,
fat particles from hamburgers and see Oh 2.
being from Lunaria i can see these things.
NASA's space elevator won't make it to Mars
or my planet either. carbon nanotubes just
too unstable. like the paths of politicians on
self-avoiding walks, pacing out probability
of market symmetry versus random calamity.
but look, the cat's eye nebula is excellent from here,
blinking cosmic secrets that i can decipher
because i am a poet from Lunaria with words
to say to anyone who wants to stay and listen.

Stephen Roxborough

dada is a verb

what is a pome is inside of your nose
        –bpNichol

At the Louvre I watch bill flick a booger onto the Mona Lisa
to see if it will set off the alarms.
        –Susan Musgrave

like dali dollars or andymat or simply
how he lovinglee
        pluckd invention   out
uv his majik mucus oozing cavity
        then tenderlee
between thumb n dexterous 4fingr rolld n needed it
in2 an impressionable per4mance projektile
        a bill uv rights 4 wise foolz
                a declaration of outside
        independence
th snotty art world hasnt witnessd since
        marcel duchamp
                drew a blasphemous stash
        on her womanly grin   had ther bin
                wun eternal collektiv jungian instant!

finger flicked n flung launched in2 space
toward her perfekt goldn frame
        in wondr in passion in ultimate silliness n childlike insite
2 prove if she behind shatterproof pane wud chime
        bells uv alarm
                like nest protecting female   or male
defending her honor   or perhaps

nothing but inaudible

(   ) splat

th famous face defaced n ooze uv bissett
disfigurd flat against thick glass
over leos impermanent first portrait ikon
2 bloody westrn uncivilization
her b guyling smile
unchangd unalterd unadulteratd
even a striking beauty mark
booger
from new world hinterlandz
cudnot shake her unvirgin
born agen serene italian transgenderd
immaculate madonna
gayz

Stephen Roxborough

lines spoken a few miles below rideau canal

brief rant about bill bissett's poetry composed by MP
Bob Wenman and delivered in parliament, december 13, 1977

this material supported and masquerading
in the name of art is a demeaning degradation
of human experience

it is in my view neither creative nor beautiful
it is not even grotesque or ugly beautiful
it is neither uplifting nor fulfilling
it is not even passionate or erotic

it is simply vulgar degradation of the human experience
vulgar and demeaning at a level well below
that of funky graffiti written on the back
of washroom doors

this type of vulgarity deserves to be placed
in a category of the hate literature of pop art
and should not be censored but rather branded
as unfit for human consumption

and discarded on the rubbish heap
to rot in its own vulgarity

Letter 2 b

I saw you last night in a video.
You were talking, reading, and giving
your rattle a kiss. You were sincere,
had something to say and do.
You had been around the block.
Old friend, companion of the way,
as Robin would say, I salute you
and your gentle shoulders.
Your large and sly intelligence.
I'd like to keep the machines out of
your way and my own way, too.
One of your paintings is on my wall
and when machines start grinding,
I look at it and hear your voice.

Yvonne Trainer

&
WHERRR LING DER VISH 4 bill

thing-king uf bill n how undurstood i feel

whn i'm ahround im

hE lIk a bru thur borne in th sAm woom uf

hU
man
it
tE

n how i wus brot out uf

mI tEEn yrs

intue

wo (hU) man hood

bI hs pOmes

thAy wr sO gud

I wuud rEEd thm n hug thm

at noonhour bEhInd mI lock-her dore

wIle   prEten ding

to Et an apul to th cOr

n lAter I met im chan ting on a stAge

in TeeO   n

his pOmes werr ull sO marvOlless n ful uf silly-bowls

of nuun still-lIfe tht I waun ted tu Et thm 4evr

fuud frm the gahds

remember you read aloud i hid

beneath the table sucked your cock
your voice nearly screamed out the last
line of the poem when you came you
reached down and grabbed my hair i
gagged i had wanted it to happen when
you read "peace makes yu paranoid/ war
makes yu dead" but i didn't i didn't even gag
let alone swallow & not to put too fine a
point on it i didn't even suck your cock i
didn't suck it ever oh bill peace made me
paranoid i confess peace made me paranoid.

driving mr. bill

I drove
the poet beside me slept
sick, fevered
do you mind?
he asked
the sleeping?
no, I told him
almost meaning it
he slept

I drove
through sagebrush, dry hills
sand dunes, parchment skies
a sleeping poet
by my side

At the place with the name
I cannot spell
'Wal-is-she/he in'
the place of dead orchards
and withered dreams
he woke and
we searched for a washroom

none was there

imagine, the poet said,
a town so small it has no
washroom
but behind those rocks, there
on the hills
as the river dips and
dizzies down, dusts down
he found a place

it worked for him
one leafy bush, two minutes
a fast zipper
and it was done

ah the poet said
climbing back into the car
stretching, smiling
then sleeping once more

next stop, Savona, I said
soon, soon, soon
and pray there will be
in Savona
a place for me and my goddess bladder
my goddess squat and deliver style

or else
beside the highway
I shall offer my backside to the sky
my thighs to
the sixteen wheelers
leering by

please
let there be
in Savona
relief for me

but
Savona
had gone

we had to pass through it

you can't get from Cache
creek
to Kam
loops
unless Savona
holds the two apart
it says so
right here on
this bcaa map
Savona
right there
see?

it wasn't there

the poet knew what had happened
poets know these things
it's brigadoon reversed
he explained, waking,
almost waking,
Cariboo brigadoon
dry dusty wind and sand
brigadoon
happens in May

once every hundred years
the town of Savona
disappears
today must be that day
isn't that excellent
isn't that truly excellent?

he sang
brigadoon, brigadoooooon
savona, savonaaaaaaaaa
then slept again

head back, neck cricked
dreaming of spirit world
of parents there
there there not here

I drove
through sunshine
and
magic rainbows
my bladder aching
while the poet snored

zzzzzzzBRIGADOONzzzzzzzzzzzzzzzzz

zzzzzzzzzzzzzzzzzzzzzzzSAVONAzzzzzzzzzzzzzzzzzzzzzzzzzz

zzzzzzzzzzzzzzzzzzzzzzzzzzzEXCELLENTzzzzzzzzzzzzzzzzzz

zzzzzzzzzzzzzzzzzzzzzzzzzzzzAHzzzzzzzzzzzzz

belt it bliss

bill:charged
is:être
set:word tables
t:n trumpets

Darren Wershler-Henry

Nightmare Anthology: The Corrected bill bissett*

I was printing bile.
The kid ate by the metal Honda. He seeks guns
from it, for it was published
by itself. We wear it like printing
in the previously occurring issue.

Shun the ultraviolet bellowing of mentors.
I was working the press, thin with Latinate Bernard.
My hair veered along
1,970 circuits, half way down my back.

I was learning how to print
with an offset bodice. I was
standing out in my ovum's garden.
Hair acute in our electric rollers,
the machines were thundering on, turning fat ultraviolet. The iceberg stops
them, theocracy in the wall.
On the room's far side, utter impiety.

I was screaming.
Bernard N. sits wed in the orchard,
looking at the friars' ova,
canines on the pig's waybills. The tress
and the riven sky ultraviolet in the breech of the levees.
No Hun came running.

They told me that afterward
I was practicing sums.
Gnu sounds patter from the distaffs.
It sounded free. Nice, they said.

Some theses have a lot of issues:
ultraviolet hair, stucco, anthems.

* This poem was produced by running bill bissett's "i was printing billy th kid"
  through Microsoft Word's spell checker.

Re: rejoice in blue hat bill

when blue hat bill leaves, there's little
balls of green gum
stuck everywhere,
and me and my little parrot both wish
blue hat bill was still here,
to chew his, *magic green things* –
so we can watch his
space rocket tongue turn
Clorette green some more
as he tells his well-seen stories
in poetry vision glory, *sanga
halleluja*, song blue hat bill sings
birdlike, to Chewchewknee and me,
amour orator, conductor
of magic trains – *whoo whoo*

when blue hat bill leaves, there are little
balls of magic green things, stuck everywhere,
as little peppermint reminders of open
sweetness, lightning and magic rainbows
spirit quest, urban gypsy dressed
oak tale mountain and rattle beat song

when blue hat bill leaves,
Chewchewknee's perplexed
confused and slightly vexed –
in the morning, instead of her usual
good morning, good morning
she says, *xcellent, xcellent,* in bill speak

she parrots him in bissett-ease; frenetic
she flies room to room
looking for her favourite friend, to resume
last night's late-night escapade caper,
blue hat bill doesn't escape her,
she'll find his funky cobalt thrill and rage
shake her tail feathers, engage
sing along to his ongoing song,
sanga halleluja

where's his magic monkey, I ask
bill, where's bill? she retracks
last night's flight patterns, where's bill?
and his angels, she looks for his angels
crystal lady, contessa, and sister barb
empress diana, doctor karl with a c
princess rosa, la d, doctor bill
and mister seagull, she looks
for all the visiting angels
blue hat bill brings –
she looks and looks
and then, I see her little parrot eyes realize
all of them have left with blue hat bill
she cries and cries –
damn it, now I'm stuck with you
my little parrot is saddened
her wings are less red somehow
she flies listless somehow

looking for and looking
for, the missing something that is missing
somehow, without bill, *where's bill?*
     she asks, *where's bill, bill?*
     madcap wingnut speed trap rap
sanga, sanga, sanga
she learns about all things seen
and space in between from blue hat bill
brushstroke feathers figure skate across
movie screens; with Anne Murray singing background jukebox
she isn't just a bird with blue hat bill
she is the sum of all things –
human, and other times beast
telepathic lover and *Canadian Geese*
street-wise confidante, sometimes
she's his son, other times the wind
bells ring she didn't know were there
blue hat bill teaches her all things –
going to spirit, dancing with god
about all things, flying
to and from the other world, all things
simple from complex take wing
magic strings, all things, blue hat bill
bissett:
two *b*'s, two *i*'s, two *l*'s, two *s*'s, two *t*'s and an *e*
for *xcellent*
xcellent, on blue birdy bill

bill bissett

bill bissett

i was born in lunaria a wundrful galaxee – planet v far away byond venus 312 manaa manee dayze n nites 2 get ther or cum from arrivd in erthling inkarnaysyun 300 erth yeers ago approx as navigaysyn assistant undr first navigaytor jonathan jonathan can intrpret erthling behavious wch i am not abul 2 he can send reports 2 lunaria uv such n same i am not abul 2 emptee tapes or disks ar put in my hed whn theyr filld they ar remoovd sent 2 lunaria well downloadid uv kours n emptee wuns ar put in makes me feel lite hedid 4 a whil i love writing n painting n dewing reedings n travelling n falling in love in seeminglee impossibul situaysyuns mos recent book from talonbooks narrativ enigma most recent see dee with bill roberts composr from red deer press rumours uv hurricane upcum-ming book from talonbooks northern wild roses wch displays n xploors th intraktivitee relaysyunships btween word n images wch is reelee part uv my lifes work n upcumming see dee from red deer deth interrupts th dansing with composr pete dako ium sew in2 sound xplooring th manee brillyanses uv langage n image love having art shows as well recent art book hand paintid from granaree books nyc lunaria an xposisyun uv th serch 2 reseev blessing kleerans from th oral aisles uv my home planet erth is sew diffikult sumtimes i just want 2 go home 2 lunaria but am reelee heer in erth as part uv a life long whatevr that meens sz implies reserch teem yes yes i try n b hopeful sumtimes thats reelee onlee an akt uv faith wch sumtimes is reelee sumthing isint it yes yes yes lunarian blessings 4 us all

sept 05

Postscript: A River Runs Through Him

M.A.C. Farrant

I gave a writing class to a group in the city. It was held one evening in the basement of a library. The idea was that I would provide writing exercises, and talk about the craft. Thirteen people were in attendance, among them an eighty-eight year old man who had just self-published his twelfth book. It was called *Travel Tales*. "It's about my thirty years in the travel business," he told the group when it was his turn during introductions. "An insider's view. Things you'd never suspect that go on behind the scenes." He had copies with him, for sale.

Another student said she had written a book on management skills and was interested in who my agent was. A shy Chinese woman said she came to the class because she was stuck in the house all day and needed something to do. A woman, who kept her coat on and her purse on her lap, said she was attending as support for her husband who wanted to write westerns. He sat next to her, tilted back in his chair, a fleshy, middle-aged man with a pencil stuck behind his ear.

While the participants worked on the first exercise – "Details from your Childhood" – the supporting wife stared grimly over her husband's shoulder at what he was writing. Beside them a lively elderly couple took turns with a pen writing on the same sheet of paper. After completing the exercise, the wife of the elderly couple told the group that she and her husband had gone to elementary school together and so shared the same childhoods. Her husband, a thin man in an oversized blue sweatshirt that had "The Right Stuff" written in white across his chest, explained their unique writing style. "We do this all the time. The wife writes the beginning of sentences and I write the end. I'm better at ends than she is."

I told the group we would now do an exercise called "Stretching the Commonplace; Blowing off the Dust." "It's about using the imagination," I said, and explained that I would provide them with a first sentence— something provocative or startling. They would then write the next sentence, and the next, moving on to paragraphs if they felt inspired. To get them going and to give them an idea of how wonderful such writing could be, I read aloud a poem by bill bissett. It began: *god or th goddess as yu like 2 say is a giant/ child leening against a giant window sill/ looking out at rolling emerald hills th shining/ turquoise watr brite yello zaneeness birds evree/ wher lifting melodeez...*

When I had finished I said, "A writer like bill bissett has the doors wide open all the time. A universe runs through him. bill bissett is in a permanent state of wonder, perfectly attuned to the swirl of life within and beyond him."

The man with the supporting wife scoffed, and said, "What's he on?"

Several people laughed.

The three sentences I gave the class to choose from were: "My mother ate cats"; "I had charge of an insane asylum, and I was insane"; and "They have lost the baby down the sewer." They had ten minutes. Then everyone shared what they had written.

Of the thirteen people in the class, eleven, including the elderly couple, had chosen sentence number one about the mother who ate cats. The shy Chinese woman chose sentence number three about losing the baby down the sewer. "We went crazy with fear," she wrote. When it was his turn to read, the man with the watching wife smirked, folded his arms across his chest, and said, "Pass."

I then talked about dreams and the other places imaginative material might be found. "It's important not to get stuck in habitual grooves," I said, thinking fondly of bill. Some of the students wrote this down.

At the end of the class, the man with the watching wife explained to everyone the proper way to sit in a chair. He said there should never be wrinkles in your wrists when you work at the computer, and that the screen should be blue, not white. He said you should get up every twenty minutes and walk around. "Move the blood. Otherwise it pools." He said he was an expert in ergonomics. That's what he did for a living.

For all this I was paid fifty dollars. The next day I took another trip to the city. I planned to spend the money at secondhand stores. I was looking for a winter sweater. Also, I needed some brite yello zaneeness.

Chronology
(linear bill: a few dates, events & people)

1939	Born November 23 in Halifax, Nova Scotia
1953	bill's mother goes to spirit
1956	Attends Dalhousie University
	Runs away from home with a preacher's son to join the circus
1958	Stops running in Vancouver, BC
1961–67	Lives with Martina Clinton
1962	Daughter Ooljah is born
1963–65	Attends University of British Columbia; meets Warren Tallman, Patrick Lane, Jim Brown, Judith Copithorne and Maxine Gadd
1963–83	Establishes blewointment magazine and press (to publish volumes by bpNichol, Steve McCaffery, Andrew Suknaski, Lionel Kearns, Maxine Gadd and d.a.levy)
1965	With Patrick Lane, Seymour Mayne and Jim Brown, forms Very Stone House
1966	First books: *fires in the tempul OR th jinx ship n othr trips* (Very Stone House/blewointment) and *we sleep inside each other all* (bpNichol's Ganglia Press)
1968	With Joy Long and Gregg Simpson, creates cooperative art gallery, Th Mandan Ghetto
	Busted taking marijuana to a Powell River commune; spends a few weeks at Oakalla Prison Farm (winter 1968–69), plus some jail time in Powell River, Vancouver and Burnaby. *awake in the red desert* (Talonbooks) released, included12" vinyl LP, with avant-garde rockers Th Mandan Massacre (named by bill; LP produced by Jim Brown)
1969	Falls 20 feet to a concrete floor at a Kitsilano house party, severely injuring his head. Warren Tallman and Gerry Gilbert read poetry to a catatonic and paralyzed bill in hospital; when bill surfaces, he has to relearn body movements and speech

1970   *Why dusint the League of Canadian Poets do sumthing nd get an organizer for cross country poetry reading circuit,* chapbook (blewointmentpress)

1971   *NOBODY OWNS TH EARTH*: bill's first collected works; poems chosen by Margaret Atwood & Dennis Lee (Anansi)

1977–78   Conservative MP Bob Wenman complains in Parliament that taxpayers subsidize pornographic poetry (through Canada Council Grants), specifically raging against bill's work

1980   *Beyond Even Faithful Legends, Selected Poems 1962-1976* (Talonbooks)

1981   European tour with Susan Musgrave: bill meets the Queen and Mona Lisa meets bill

1982   *READY FOR fRAMINg* (blewointmentpress), 20 b&w prints in an edition of 300

1984   *fires in th tempul:* Solo Art Exibition, Vancouver Art Gallery

1985–86   Writer-in-Residence, University of Western Ontario, London

1989   Group Show: *Reasoning,* Vancouver Art Gallery; London, Ont. rock band Luddites, release 12" vinyl LP; bill is lyricist and singer; 1990 Milton Acorn People's Poet Award

        Why I write like ths poetree is for communikaysyun, essay (Poetry Canada Review)

1993   Dorothy Livesay BC Book Award for Poetry (*inkorrect thots*); Creative Writing teacher, York University, Toronto

1997   *The Capilano Review* 25th anniversary issue devoted to bill, edited by Patrick Friesen and Sharon Thesen in concert with a bill tribute at the Vancouver Writers Festival

1998   Writer-in-Residence with Carol Malyon, University of New Brunswick, Fredericton

2000   Writer-in-Residence, Capilano College, North Vancouver

2001   *Lunaria* published by Steve Clay (Granary Books); handpainted edition of 40

2003   Dorothy Livesay BC Book Award for Poetry (*peter among th towring boxes*)

2004   *The Writing Is on the Wall,* exhibition & performance of bill's concrete poetry, curated by Lenore Herb, and "Writing Inside Writing" paper on bill presented by Dr. Carl Peters (Kootenay School of Writing, Vancouver)

Sandra Alland – Ever since our trip to Allan Gardens, we've been the best of friends. If bill's wisdom and humour could be bottled, anti-depressants might be unnecessary.

Margaret Atwood – The picture reference in "Astral Twin" is the tenth image from the front in bill's book *lunaria*. I used it as a signpost when writing my novel *Oryx and Crake*. bill bissett is my astral twin. Same year, same month, same day. The connection might not be immediately obvious, but think about it really hard and after a long time you will get an insight. We're both Scorpios. They take strange forms. Obverse and reverse. If you count all the letters in our first and last names, taking "bill" as "William," each total is 14, which is – numerologically speaking – a 5. (Freedom and the five senses, say some.) Apart from that, let's just say I met bill at a "happening" back in 1964. I felt something furry crawling between my legs. It was bill. (Why be surprised? In the Chinese horoscope, we're both rabbits.) At one point I put together a best-of-bill for House of Anansi Press, from stacks and stacks of blewointments (*NOBODY OWNS TH EARTH*). It's the sort of thing you do for an astral twin.

Leanne Averbach – bill bissett is a man outland that lets all in. I first worked with him when he was writer-in-residence at the Capilano College Writing Program. He presided over his tiny office with enough warmth and generosity to make many, including me, feel excellent. bill is lit with heart and drumbeat that makes me feel mad with gentleness, words.

Margaret Avison – One morning, during library days, I vividly remember. Spring, a frantic season on campus, and bp [Nichol] elatedly cried "Come out! A friend from Vancouver is outside! You've got to meet!" He and I and bill bissett sat in the sunny triangle of grass (northeast of the old building, now the Medical Library) and again, all the essentials were in place. bill's *th influenza uv logik* later showed the mutuality in that buoyant friendship language. bill had a capacity for suffering, and bp for compassionate wholeness. Together they were discovering their own freedom of word and gesture. (Excerpt from *Where the Words Come From: Canadian Poets in Conversation*. Ed. Tim Bowling, interview by Sally Ito. Nightwood, 2002.)

Kemeny Babineau – "Phenhomona 3B" is sound and vision buzzing into the multifarious dance of the many. bill's poetry has always taught me, when we restrict ourselves foolishly to choices of either/or, we reduce our world into binary units, static division. That's not where the life is. Life is in poetry, and not just as literature, but as being three: free, be 3, live the phenomena.

Elizabeth Bachinsky – I was in grade 9 when I first picked one of bill's books off the library shelf and, as his letters leapt off the page, I remember thinking *whoa, this is totally awesome*. Fifteen years later, whenever I feel frightened or unsure about writing what I think or feel, I think of bill and all the work he's done, and continues to do, to make it possible for writers in this country to think and speak and publish without self-censorship. A little while ago, I started a reading series in my hometown. bill came out to read. Understand, Maple Ridge is a conservative town... but bill packed the house. There was an elderly woman sitting directly in front of bill as he read. bill was hot, he was raging: *i dont want 2 suck any empire, i just want 2 suck yu*... and there was this little lady – she had to be in her late eighties – chuckling away in the first row as if his reading was the best thing she'd ever heard. That's what I find most inspiring about bill: he doesn't hold back, and his courage is contagious. bill crosses boundaries again and again which is something all writers – especially poets – should do. So I look to bill for guidance. How wonderful that he has met so many younger poets as friends. It's not often you get to meet your heroes, but it's even rarer when you do and realize they are as generous as you could have hoped.

Nelson Ball – "I've Never Seen a Mountain" was written in 1970 or 1971, when bill lived in Vancouver and I lived in Toronto. bill was an unstoppable force, cranking out issues of the now legendary *blewointment* magazine, singing peace and love, raging against social injustice, and re-envisioning the role of the League of Canadian Poets. I saw my poem as a small tribute to bill.

Douglas Barbour – "a note for bill" refers to an early encounter at Poet & Critic '69, held at the University of Alberta. We were all younger then. Earle Birney attended, Dorothy Livesay was teaching here and Elizabeth Brewster was working in the library. bill gave one of his whirl-wind performances and Elizabeth wrote a poem about it, which Stephen Scobie and I first published in a special issue of our little broadsheet *The Merry Devil of Edmonton*. In her poem she referred to his golden glow, how very different he was from poets like her, and how she admired that in him. I also remember a later visit to the university, when he danced and chanted in a large classroom, turning it into some kind of other place where shamanism still worked.

John Barlow – a common phenomenon with geniuses and bill bissett is how crazily intelligent they are – that spirit in the opening bars of "Shaft" (Isaac Hayes just springs forth with bissettness). it leaves one thinking: who will be the last Beatle? Paul or Ringo ~ bill!

Rhonda Batchelor – All encounters with bill in the last thirty years have been fun. During our last meeting, when I was purchasing some of his art/pome cards to carry in my bookshop, I was having trouble doing math in my head as we tried to figure out totals/discounts etc. bill was amazing – a regular human calculator! Who knew?! Right brain, left brain… it's all excellent.

Jill Battson – bill has always been a great friend, someone to call up and complain to about the state of the world, debate the latest film or moan about the vagaries of a lover. He's one of those people you can pick up a conversation with after not seeing for a while and it feels like it has been uninterrupted. Wherever he is on the planet, he always has time for a chat.

bill bissett – i need mor time 2 remembr lets see billy who i hitch hiked 2 vancouvr with 58 we wer 2gethr ovr 2 yeers hfx n van thn manee currents lostnesses findings heer ther th roads street manee hiwayze thn martina i think that wd b 61 yes til 67 thn bertrand 69–72 thn michael 1 74–81 thn manee events allianse not live withs xcellenses as alwayze michael 2 96–99 thn with all thees xcellenses continuing reelee th last few yeers as a singul prson veree kool a few almosts undrstanding tho that singulness is as xcellent tho now paradoxikalee beleev ium bettr konstruktid 4 living with sum wun uv kours th long standing mr gull ovr 10 yeers now n what els things ar always not like b4 alwayze nu thees datyes ar approx n iklusiv uv brek ups phases prhaps who can know aneeway ium grateful 4 all uv thees brillyant xperiences n 2day n 2nite sew xcellent mor as it cums in reelee big nus cumming thers sew much utside our control i dont evn like it thats partlee why i meditate as well as it feels gud xcellent i feel sew xcellent n like sortuv smooth sailing well thats not trew i feel sew next i gess ts all sew weird wch can b xcellent ium workin on projekts xcellent still feel veree sad abt janet leigh may she rock 4evr n b always blessd ium not a big fan uv mortalitee maybe nowun is i usd 2 like it bettr i gess thats kinda strange well i gess thats all fr now from heer ar we lillipushyans transplantis lunarians living among who knows what can we b lovd n blessd n totalee happee is that asking 2 much 2nite i know ium happee i can dew my work wch i love or putting it anothr way i can dew my love wch i work limitaysyuns uv binaree abstrakt nouns ar boundless all best

George Bowering – bill bissett is a one-man culture, who bridges the apparent gap between the distant past and the farthest planets. He is a sound poet through whom spirit talks, and a primary political force for our shared good. He is a lesson for us all…

Di Brandt – I lived in bill's apartment for a winter once, maybe that's when his poetic voices began seeping into me. writing a pome for bill in his inimitable style has ruined me for life, my hands refyuse to spell things properlee aneemore, and i keep breaking out in sillee jokes n profetic rants in strange playces evrywun shd trye it   it brings out the wild in u   hey bill can't imagine canada or poetree w out u   good on ya   keep it up   yeah

Alice Breeze – I had the pleasure of meeting bill at "Poetry on the Rocks" in Kimberley, BC. One of the most wonderful days in my life. Everyone who knows bill would agree: bill is love.

Brian Brett – So many things to say about bill… bill is bill. That's always been more than enough for me. If bill claims he never met the bear, just tell him he forgot, or better yet, that every song should have one good lie in it.

Jim Brown – I never did see the bulldozers but bill and Martina moved to a flat above the Salvation Army on 4th Avenue where they continued their adventurous lifestyle and their combined efforts putting out *blewointment* magazine and blewointment books. Putting together the Mandan Ghetto art gallery with Joy Long led them to form a performance band and to record bill's *awake in th red desert* album with th Mandan Massacre as bill's backup band. We recorded it at the new electronic music lab at UBC in the music department building and it was probably the best session I produced, even though it was one of the first. Three decades later, some young guys in Florida bought one of the vinyl albums for $800 on the internet and got in touch with bill and me and we cut a deal with them for it to be made into a CD available from Gear/Fab Records: http://www.swiftsite.com/gearfab/.

I performed "Th Very Tissues of Language" during the time bill was in jail and in the hospital, and then I continued to perform it after he got out of the hospital and Sid Simons got him his get out of jail free card. This took place during a very turbulent period of '60s history in Kitsilano when the narks had it in for bill because they saw him as some sort of cult leader, which he never really was. bill was just bill, a shaman chanting his beatific self to the winds. He was a seminal force in small magazine publishing but he was no threat. He didn't have a political agenda. I guess they resented his street sense and his detached non materialist attitude. In retrospect, I guess they didn't like the way he dressed, either. bill was a painter, too, and his images, such as the ones he chose to illustrate my first book *The Circus in the Boy's Eye* often offended people such as my wife and her shrink. They thought that the image of a man kissing a woman's breast in the frontispiece was somehow done on purpose to threaten her, dear girl, and they both told me so. The '50s were a desperate repressive era and in the '60s we were just beginning to colour outside the lines, that's all, and authority figures everywhere wanted to shut all of us down. That's what "Th Very Tissues of Language" is about. More than anybody, the authority figures wanted to shut bill bissett down and I chose to speak out on his behalf. Probably more than anybody other than Warren Tallman in those days bill bissett helped me to set myself free.

John Burgess – I first performed with bill at a small community arts centre in Abbotsford, BC, with rox and Matt Gano. "3 transmissions" comes from conversations we had during the drive from Vancouver. We talked about string theory, movies, typewriters vs. word processors and setting tabs. But what has remained with me the most since then is bill's disarming openness. It unclogs, inspires, liberates.

Steve Clay – When I met bill the first thing I noticed was his complete openness to whomever and whatever. Period. He keeps opening more and spreads enormous generosity wherever he goes. I was initially taken aback but quickly realized – this is the way it is supposed to be. bill is one of the great spiritual teachers of our time and our realm. I count meeting him and working together to publish his book *lunaria* great highlights of my work at Granary. The moment recounted in the poem was sparked by one example of the radiance of bill's continuous generosity.

Mark Cochrane – bill, Adeena Karasick and I launched books together in 2000, and when I read "Sexing the Page" bill was sitting in the front row. I followed up the poem, nerdishly, by reassuring the audience that of course this never happened, nobody ever jerked me off onto one of bill's old manuscripts of typographic concrete. "That's too bad," bill said. He sounded sad for me and not ironic.

j.d. crosato – I wrote a pome for bill called "ucudntcumtumy-brthdyprtywhn" and gave bill a copy. I wondered whether he had read it, so I wrote "near forgotten phantasms." On the surface the pome says, "Hey bill, about that pome I built for you, did you read it yet? I filled it up with memories of your majik and your eyes." Some lines end with the word "bill," but the word is simultaneously the first word for the next line. The word "bill" can mean mistr bill, and mean bill/did (builded/built), at the same time. bill's magic helps him connect with the marvellous imaginings of the world and communicate those wonders through the special way he uses intuition, voice and language. He is a physical phenomenon which exists partially outside the limits of the five accepted sensory channels.

j ocean dennie – The inspiration for "annihilation uv p om" comes simply from the life and work of bill. From the moment I first laid eyes on him in the late '90s, I was hooked. There is no doubt bill lives in a very special world, a world that bill paints for us not just through poetry but through the way he leads his life. bill is "raging" all the time. He stands at the precipice of his mind every moment of the waking day. bill's writing is the kind of stuff that will inspire folks long after he's gone to say, "Holy shit, yeah, I get it now! Wow! That's absolutely amazing! Yeah, look at how he did that! Huh! How about that! Unbelievable…"

John Donlan – I wrote "Shedden" to commemorate a road trip we made when bill was writer-in-residence at the University of Western Ontario. He later created a construction that included photos from the trip, which I bought from him, and it revives fond memories of a happy day with my friend.

Paul Dutton – After attempting a lipogram excluding all letters but those in the name *bill bissett*, I decided to add the exclamatory *oh*, which not only broadened the verbal field considerably, but struck me as a fitting title for a poem in a book such as this. The poem's content is fictional, of course, but here are a few facts that I know about bill: his trademark *brilliant* and *excellent* started in the '80s, prior to which his phatic terms of choice had been groovy and far out; he can charm everyone sitting within chatting distance on a plane to the UK or a train in England; and when a Montreal power failure interrupts a poetry reading, he doesn't need the substituted candlelight for his portion of the evening, having committed to memory enough of his poetry for the occasion.

Cathy Ford – First met the work of bill bissett in my high school library and realized immediately he was, and is, most positively, politically, humanly, alive of all poets so far read, reading ahead, writing, spelling, transformative, before all. Amazing he is still: keeping us humble, revolutionizing. Knew there was a poem in this sensibility about bill bissett's influence on my own work as a poet, just did not know until it began that the very poem was this one, "the opening of the mouth ceremony." So there a door again opens, or is it a window? Thanks to bill bissett, himself, and all like-minded, as ever, grateful.

Patrick Friesen – An accumulation of memories and images went into "white horse." I remember, when I still lived in Winnipeg, having a discussion about Billy Eckstine's voice while listening to a CD of bill's. I've also heard certain vocal techniques of Nina Simone's that may well have influenced bill at one point or another. And, for some reason, when I first moved to Vancouver I had an image of bill riding a white horse through the intersection of Burrard and Davie, and he was riding toward the sea.

Maxine Gadd – Would be glad to remind bill of the time he visited and grabbed a bunch of pages. I was sick with something devastating and couldn't chase him. He soon after published a book he titled *hochelaga* after some history I'd been reading. I still like the book and bill. Isn't it good to have ratched spelling, like when you lose the drift to get to the desired stream?

Candis Graham – I first met bill at a wedding ceremony for mutual friends in Vancouver. One of our shared roles was to stand by the garden gate and greet guests. There is a photograph of us, in our wedding duds, chewing red twists of licorice. "from one drama queen/to another" came from my memories of that scrumptious evening. I've been using his poems to inspire writers in my workshops for years.

Heidi Greco – "th most xcellent picknik" is based on one of the first times I met bill. The music in bissett's poems has had an influence on my own work, as has his obvious reverence for all things both living and gone to spirit. For those gifts, and for other joys he's shown me, I am grateful.

Jane Eaton Hamilton – hey mamas, of course you remember, mamas. I was a very mischievous baby, don't you remember that? and irascible. lots of fun. showed signs of gayness at a very early age. you remember that, and realizing that was excellent? I was really good at drawing and writing and not very good at anything else of a scholastic nature. I'm sure you remember those things. I always pulled your hair a lot and jumped on you. yes? okay, excellent. of course, mamas, I love you lots. I weighed 12 pounds 8 ounces at birth. I didn't take to school. don't you remember these things, mamas? I guess you're getting on a bit. remember how I didn't take to sports, either, except ballet? excellent. I didn't do ballet from birth. I did it a little while after birth. my doctors still worry about me growing taller. I'm taller a little bit more this year than last year. this may not be excellent because it may stretch organs. oh! well! excellent! so I love you both very, very much. why haven't you come to rescue me from various stuff? mamas are supposed to… excellent.

Pauline Holdstock – I came to Canada from England in the 1970s. bill bissett was the first Canadian poet I met, a radiant sign that this was not a land of RCMP officers after all. "Considering bill," is a short pome with apologies to Christopher Smart's (1722–1771) "Jubilate Agno." Smart is believed to have written the poem during his extended confinement in a madhouse. The manuscript did not come to light until the 1930s. "Rejoice in the Lamb," perhaps better known by its first line "For I will consider my cat Jeoffry," enumerates seventy-four felicities of the cat, probably an excellent means of preserving sanity.

Geoff Inverarity – For me, the time you spend with bill is like the time you spend with his poetry – you're constantly slipping between realities, transcending the sensible world in explosions of cosmic vision, and I'm thankful for bill and the portals he opens. Every time the phone rings and you hear, "hi, are you raging?" I settle in, put down what I'm doing, whatever it is, because bill's about to transform my day. We're going exploring. There will be lightning and magic rainbows and it's always been far too long since we went on one of these journeys.

Ellen S. Jaffe – I first met bill bissett when he was writer-in-residence at the Woodstock Public Library in Woodstock, Ontario (1987–88). He created a writing group in the library basement. bill's excitement, encouragement, enthusiasm, got me writing again in a new way. I read bill's poems often, and took his books or poems with me when I was away from home. One night, my son and I visited friends in Toronto and slept in a room with glowing plastic stars on the ceiling. It was another time of change in my life, and after reading one of bill's poems and looking at the stars, I experienced one of those moments of illumination, when things just ARE and life becomes clear and good in the moment, without trying to make rationale sense of it.

Kedrick James – I was directing the production of "Planet Poetry" for Bravo TV in Vancouver at a West End house bill was sharing. In the nervous chaos of filmmaking, bill was welcoming, calm, and beneficent with tea and kind words for the frenzied crew around him. No one was left out or extraneous to the glow of his person. We shot a little bit but decided at the last minute we needed a different setting for his performance sequence. We chose a rooftop pool, and being so encumbered with gear, it got quite late into the night by the time we transported everything and everybody to the new location. The pool was dark and the walkway dangerous with cords and wires. Finally the lighting and sound and cameras were ready and bill was lit against a starry background of Vancouver and English Bay. He looked radiant, like a prophet just descended from the sky. His performance was magical, incredibly moving, heart-wrenching yet playful, joyous and sad. It was a gift. He transcended all the cameras and gear, as if it were meant to happen that way. He completed his takes and we took bill home. It was early in the morning and bill was exhausted, but he still cheered us on and skipped to his bed. With anyone else, the experience would likely have been a disaster. With bill it was as though nothing could go wrong. It is his unique blessing, that feeling when you're around him, there is goodness in the world and he is a messenger come to give you a sample.

Karl E. Jirgens – "bill bissett, a photo-portrait" is based on the time bill and I were in Montreal at the Ultimatum Festival. I was doing double duty because, like bill, I'd been invited to read, but I was also researching a book on bill for ECW (*Bill Bissett and His Works*). I had my camera and tape recorder. After doing our own gigs and tuning in to a stint of readings, bill and I took a break from the fest and headed for a bistro. It was cold that day – I had dressed too lightly and bill lent me his jean jacket with the cut-off sleeves. We talked while the tape rolled. Eventually, hunks of the interview ended up in the book and *Rampike* (13/2, "For the Record: An Interview with bill bissett" pp. 10-13). bill talked about his art, his family history, his denunciation by the House of Commons for his notorious poem "awarmplacetoshit," the culture heroes who leapt to his defence, and his efforts to earn a living by chopping wood or washing dishes, so that he could keep doing his art. He also talked candidly about literary influences, editing blewointment press, his head injury and the cosmic experience that resulted. I've always been impressed by his sensitivity and humanity, his intelligence and his knowledge of literature. Beyond being a prolific and important artist, bill's a natural healer, inspired by an astral impulse. He doesn't hesitate to point out the bogus sides of society, but always balances acerbic observations by citing something beautiful. Anyway, I took a photo of bill performing, and the poem-portrait I wrote spun out of that. The photo happened decades ago, as did the interview – but, the poem happened in a flash when I heard about this book in honour of bill.

Adeena Karasick – . . . and then there was the time, when we got chased by a wicked witch in Oxford, forced to dance around the Montague; chant sound poetry until the sun came up; when we almost drowned on a hydrofoil from Osten to Dover; when we got locked in the National

Museum in Berlin by Gestapo police; when you read *lunaria* in my living room; when we were up all nite doing shrooms in the raven kastul, through deaths and divorces and births and eye pus and burning feet, tooth drilling hemorrhoids, hypoglycemia and hypochondria, unkul bill you have been there for me and every day u remind me how words are magical creatures, how everything is a series of misrepresentations, projections, veils, appearances, specters; how we live inside language, and create our world through it. remind me how to play with your luggage is to play with your baggage, how language is music, is always disappearing, enigmatic, out of reach but is filled with the uncanny and explodes into desire, an erotic arena of possibility. And i feel so incredibly blessed for this gift of proximity, fullness, of aching beauty, magic and complexity (and each of these terms not transcendental metaphysical empty signifiers but are inscribed with particularity, a singularity which redoubles itself in this telling). and every day, i remain, forever impacted, forever grateful.

Bob Kasher – bill has always struck me as one of the most amazing writers and artists i've ever met because bill doesn't just write and paint, he lives and breathes his art in everything he is and does. his commitment to his message is astonishing and his message is beautiful, embracing and encompassing all races, orientations and creeds. as such, he is to me more than a person, he is an archetype and possibly the most important artist this young country has yet produced for his unswerving devotion to his vision and for the beauty of that vision.

Penn Kemp – The first part of a "Certain Chance Chant" is an homage to bill's blewointment press. The second is an homage to bill himself. After a joint reading at Toronto's Pteros Gallery, bill and I taped a raucous duet, performing my "poem for peace in two voices" at PsychoSpace Sound Studios. This little poem has been translated into eighty-six languages and will be included on my CD *Poem for Peace in Many Voices*.

Beth Kinar – i was the youngest of six siblings. as a child i loved writing and poetry. in my twenties i was a cocktail waitress and flirt and didn't write a bit. in my thirties i married, had kids and a dog and didn't write a bit. in my forties, through tragedy, my friend Stephen encouraged me to write and introduced me to the amazing mr bill bissett. since then, i have continued my attempts. i have had the pleasure of hosting two raging poetry parties at our home featuring bill and other wonderful poets. poetry has helped me find a piece of myself that had been missing, and bill has inspired me to continue the search.

Tim Lander – I wish I had more time to meditate on bill's billness. He's the best we've got.

Patrick Lane – bill and I go a long way back to 1962 or '63. May he travel singing forever.

Scott Lawrance – When I think about bill my thoughts return to those collective spaces of the elusive, oft-maligned and mythologized days of the '60s. My very first memory of him was wandering into the Sound Gallery, a co-operatively run space where musicians (especially Al Neil trio, with Gregg Simpson and Rick Anstey), visual artists and others (e.g. Sam Perry, Gary Lee-Nova) brought forward a dazzling and generative matrix of energy. bill was reading/chanting and the closest comparison my suburban mind could come at that time was the sexual and politically provocative image of early Mick Jagger. But bill was of THIS place, of these weathers and landforms, and his voice, his singing was an ageless connection to roots that I didn't even know I had. In those very beginnings, despite the darkness and tragedies that informed our lives in those days, bill was such a central figure in setting a brilliant direction for himself and so many others, even as he was being himself formed and shaped by that community, not least of which was, of course, Martina and Ooljah, which is self-evident but deserves saying.

d.a. levy – "i thot th world uv d.a.levy thn n now i still dew love n admire him sew much n his work sew brillyant we wrote each othr all th time back n forth from th beginning uv our literaree frendship   prob ablee abut wuns a week we each wrote each othr   thru him uv kours i met jim lowell uv th asphodel book shop also thru th mail onlee who went 2 spirit veree recentlee   d.a. or daryl n i wrote each othr from cleveland 2 vancouvr 2 cleveland always whn did i first bgin publishing him in blewointment press veree erlee an ode 2 d.a.levy was part uv my book n record *awake in th red desert* it was part uv thos projekts in 68 i think he was in th same issew as whn bwp first printid bpNichol yes 65   th nite he went 2 spirit I was on acid n i wantid 2 phone him i was veree stond n i went down th street 2 th pay phone i didint have a phone wher i was living thn in a studio ware hous got th call thru a frend uv his answerd n told me he had shot himself hours b4 i calld i went home in a dayze n lit a fire n stared in2 th fire most uv th nite praying silentlee 4 him n 4 claritee in what wer veree troubuld times in wch aneewun dewing aneething diffrent was totalee houndid th citee uv cleveland had cawsd him sew much troubul sew i nevr got 2 meet him was ths 69 printing *zen konkreet* his amayzing brillyant book i cried a lot as we had always wantid 2 hang 2gethr n crying 4 that 4 him n sew manee wreckd dreems uv sew manee at that time"

Carol Malyon – "illuminasyun" is based on a painting of the same name by bill, 1992. The face is ancient: a North American shaman perhaps, or an Aztec. The face appears to have a painted design. A jewel at the throat, perhaps another on the forehead, or a third eye. How does bill achieve this effect in a painting that consists only of a red background and lavender lines? The beholder can decide or not decide, while being pulled into the endless space beyond the lines.

Steve McCaffery – The method of my "false portrait" is exactly that – a portrait that is, to some extent, in accurate. My hope was that the slippage would not be taken literally. They'll be some felicitous appositions and some outright inaccurate. I recall the time bill actually did meet the Queen at a reception in Ottawa of artists under forty. bpNichol and Michael Ondaatje were there too and Michael noted a person in a wheelchair at the end of the line. Remembering Her Majesty's penchant for people with disabilities, he called bill and Beep over to stand by him (or her). There was also a security problem of some kind and the Queen was there for much longer than planned. Mr. Ondaatje's ploy worked and the Queen paused to talk. One signature phrase of bill's got a wondrous ovation: "Far out your Majesty!"

Kay McCracken – In June 2003 bill was a featured poet at the inaugural Shuswap Lake International Writers' Festival. "Excellent, excellent," echoed throughout hotel halls as bill's enthusiasm for life boomeranged off walls and into the hearts of us all. Not long after the festival, bill called to say he'd like to come back for a visit with a friend. During his short stay that summer, several of us found ourselves swimming in the Shuswap River.

Susan McMaster – met bill saw bill wuz amazd and overcum by bill at a leeg uv poets meeting in vancoovr. bill and frenzeed frenz were th band, ther muz n muzik marvellus wild orijinal, and MY, did we DANZ!! hav seen herd red him many times sintz, but that first enthrallment continuz 2 buzz throo my own muzik and wordz tho in very diffrunt wayz. dont think bill wood mind…

Marianne Micros – Everyone who knows bill has adventures with him. I really did dream that bill was Elvis, then himself, that he had a double, and that I wrote a poem about it. "A Dream Poem About bill bissett Cooking" is my attempt to recapture it after I woke up. When I was a teenager, Elvis was a symbol of my desire for freedom from the world of rules and gender bias of the 1950s. bill, too, is a model for me: I want to be his double, to live my life as spontaneously and creatively as he does – but I can only watch, after all, through that small window that allows me to delight in his movements as he writes and paints, defying all those rules that many of us feel compelled to follow. I can only find that spontaneity in my own life by writing poems.

Jay MillAr – I met bill in the early '90s when he was living in London Ontario. I attended a reading he gave at the central library that both frightened and amused me. In checking out bill's work in the university library I discovered blewointmentpress, his publishing empire, and realized that anyone could be a publisher. A few months later my first small press started, and since then has developed into the self-proclaimed publishing empire known as BookThug. When I think of the early work of bissett, I think of the small record that is included with *medicine my mouth's on fire*. bill's reading style on that recording is very different from what has become his style now – all the poems are read in a calm, even voice that reads his poems more than it performs them. When I think of poems like "th canadian" and of bill's books published by blewointment, I think of that voice calmly saying what it needs to say.

gustave morin – "somebody owns the earth" is a playfully irreverent recasting of one of bissett's bromides, brought up from one era and into our own, where what's obvious is simply admitted. somebody most indeed does own the earth. It touches upon the have/have not economics that bill addresses in his more overtly political poems. when one thinks of concrete poetry in canada, particularly, that rare sub-idiom known to a handful of aficionados as "dirty concrete," one can't help but closely connect this activity to the work of one man and that man is bill bissett. thank you bill, for your many wonderful contributions that have made canada a so much more interesting place to be from.

Wendy Morton – In October 2003 I had business in Edmonton and discovered bill was going to be there too. So we made a date. I was late, he was early. It didn't matter. I wanted to have a leisurely afternoon with him. He was in a hurry to get to Canmore and wanted me to go to the bus station with him. As we ate lunch at the Sunterra, he went around convincing patrons to persuade me to go to the bus station. It turned into a bill bissett event. He eventually made it to the bus station and to Canmore, where his reading was advertised for the day before.

Susan Musgrave – At the Church of Spiritual Healing we climb the blue staircase, kneel before the blue bear on the altar, the starfish on the altar cloth. bill gets a message from a Hindu in a green robe, through Mrs. Peel, the healer, whose people were taken in caravans from their land of red rain, long ago. Mrs. Peel says there is a question in bill's life. I get a message on my palm, a red wound, a stigmata. bill sees it and touches it – a miracle! bill will be cured, too: no more parasites! I light a prayer paper and a little cloud goes up. "Blessings can go through walls," bill says. (Excerpt from "When We Get There Can I Smoke?" *The Capilano Review* #23, 1997)

bpNichol – if i have a general theme it's the language trap that runs through the centre of everything i do. in this regard bill bissett first pointed the direction with a poem called "they found th wagon cat in human body." hence style is disregarded in favour of reproduction of actual states of mind in order to follow these states thru the particular traps they become in search of possible exits. hence for me there is no discrepancy to pass back and forth between trad poetry, concrete poetry, sound poetry, film, comic strips, the novel or what have you in order to reproduce the muse that muses up my own brain. —bpNichol, *Contemporary Poets of the English Language*, ed. Tosalie Murphy (St. James, 1970), p. 798.

P.K. Page – I worked at the Lampert workshops in Toronto with bill, lo, these many years ago. I also read him and love him.

Carl Peters – bill has never won the GG award and that's a crime. he, along with bpNichol and George Bowering among othrs, invented radical canadian postmodern literature. hard to beleev bissett hasnt won th GG. think uv all his books. think uv his countless incredible small press publications and ephemera and think uv his readings, his cds, th paintings, all th blewointments. think uv his incredible life in letters think uv his unstoppable spirit his love uv his fellow person poet painter searcher wonderer. he's earned admiration love and respect all over th globe. he's our best. that's hard not 2 beleev. "my name is/ bill i cum from a dysfunsksyunal specees look th /stars passing in th nite" ("hard to beleev")

Jeff Pew – 4-day editing rendezvous with rox in Vancouver. Upgraded to corner-view room at the Sylvia overlooking English Bay. 7th floor, room 27. Most auspicious. Gertrude Stein, bill's literary heroine, held salons in Paris. Her street number: 27. Her walls adorned with Picasso, Gauguin, Renoir, Cezanne and others. Ours with bissett's. Like Stein's late-night salons, room 727 was awake much of the night, with poetry, politics and musings with new and old friends. Crossed continents in bottles of red. Drapes billowed from evening bay breeze. bill at 2 am: "this is sew gatsby, aaaahhhh…. and for th moment, thay dreemed thay had evreething theyd evr need…" And we did.

Ross Priddle – "writing thru: *pass th food release th spirit book*": first i entered a trance-like state: well no, first i went and got bill's *pass th food release the spirit book* off the shelves at the local college: i read it slowly, one day at a time: then i entered a trance-like state, sat down and read/wrote my way thru the first thirty or so pages: letting each page speak and recording the "song" :::

Randy Resh – "MR blissett" is derived from my conversations with bill on the subject of magic. The role of poet as magician. ARTiculation of the ineffable. The Mage as a vehicle of the creative will. mistr bill is beyond the bounds of books & bells. Most importantly – he LIVES the royal art. That is why, incidentally, the "MR" is also short for "Master." Some of the occult philosophy underlying the poem is inspired by Aleister Crowley's The Book of the Law: "For pure will, unassuaged of purpose and delivered from the lust of result is in every way perfect," & "Do what thou wilt shall be the whole of the law."

Linda Rogers – Famously rumoured to be my former fiancé, but always our friend, our darling bill sleeps in his own room with his monkey at our house. Both of them chew magic green things, the sap and leaves of chica trees rendered into gum. The magic green is calming. I never know where I will find it after they leave – on the mirror, under the mattress, stuck in my hair, that parting kiss. Monkey and bill are tricksters. They come and go. The gum changes shape. It becomes love offerings. No one deserves our love more than our darling mistr bill.

Mari-Lou Rowley – A self-avoiding walk is a mathematical tool used in probability theory. It is similar to a random walk (another model often described as a drunkard's walk home) only it can't retrace steps or cross the same path. Over 20 percent of the aerosols above any urban centre are by-products of cooking meat. The ozone has a hard time breaking them down because of their wax-like consistency. NASA wants to build a space elevator out of carbon nanotubes to ferry electromagnetic vehicles carrying people, payloads and power between Earth and space. I can't remember the first time I heard bill read but he was raging. Our planets have aligned on several occasions. At the Glass Slipper in Vancouver before it burnt down. At the gallery above This Ain't the Rosedale Library in Toronto, where he read me the most excellent poem, freshly drafted and full of quantum leaps, cosmic details and poetic insight. At Charlie and Sarah's for Christmas brunch. And at a hotel in Seattle. bill was checking out and I was checking in as the universe continued to unfold.

Stephen Roxborough – Was the Mona Lisa really Leonardo's self-portrait in drag? Did Marcel Duchamp subconsciously reveal this, when he drew a mustache on her upper lip? What primal urges lurk inside every action, every line, every squiggle of paint? Fame, money, sex or voice, change, love? Why do artists channel the spirit of collective unconscious? Duchamp said, "Can one make works which are not works of art?" Dali said, "Those who do not want to imitate anything, produce nothing." Warhol said, "Art is what you can get away with." bissett said, "th face in th heart is th blood." How many dimensions has bill revealed? Is bill the galaxy's greatest Dada Zen master? Instead of arrows he uses unconditional love and boogers. bill's friends are among the fortunate few shown how to play inside and out, and eventually through the strings of our universe.

Yvonne Trainer – Over the years, I've had the opportunity to hear bill read several times in Toronto and Vancouver. Recently, he came to read at a bookstore in a prairie city where I lived and of course I was the first person there. After the reading a woman who is a sessional lecturer (and old enough to know better) started in on bill, using her female charms to entice him to read to her class next day. bill had to be in another city four hours away the next evening and was already tired. But he was being polite. She kept at him so long the bookstore clerks started to dim the lights. He asked how he was to get there. Would she send someone to pick him up? She said, "NO, I have to teach a class just before the next one, so you can take the bus or train." I heard my own voice like thunder. I asked her why she hadn't arranged for her students to come to the bookstore reading. I asked her if Northrop Frye were alive and came to give a talk or, if Margaret Atwood appeared for a reading in the city, would she simply waltz up and ask them to come to her class to read for free? I told her if she agreed to pay bill for the reading, and bill agreed to read, I would drive across town to the university, wait for him, take him for lunch after, and then drive him back downtown to catch the Greyhound. bill said something about not being able to read for under $75, and the whole occasion became a real hoot. We then started bartering for $100, $125, $150, $175, $200, $300, $400, $500. . . At the point we started chanting "bill b for $1000!" She suddenly looked scared and butt-ended it out of there. bill phoned later that night to thank me. I am now his unofficial agent and official built-like-a-boxer 5′ 5″ protector.

Tom Walmsley – In Vancouver about thirty years ago nearly everyone wanted to fuck bill, men and women alike. He gave such an amazing performance when he read and had a charisma you wanted to rub up against. I already loved his poetry and have a weakness for being sexually attracted to either sex if their work really grabs me. His did and does.

Ann Walsh – I live and write in the interior of BC. bill visits this region often, and I have had the pleasure of driving him to a number of conferences and workshops. The time Savona disappeared was one of the most memorable of those trips, but transporting bill anywhere is always an adventure.

Michael Dylan Welch – bill bissett continues to politely blow the tops off people's heads. Whenever I've encountered a new and typically inimitable book of his, it would say to me, "Hey, this is not your granny's poetry (nor your Governor General's)," and I would head home with a few less loonies and toonies in my pocket – but richer for it. My poem "belt it bliss" is purely wordplay (starting with an anagram), applying just one aspect of bill's uninhibited poetry. bill's is an infectious spirit!

Darren Wershler-Henry – I hate Microsoft Word. It wants me to write like a fucking accountant. The first thing I did when I loaded Office 95 onto my computer was to turn off all the auto-correct features. This poem was produced by running bill bissett's "i was printing billy th kid" through Word's spell checker, and is a pretty good indication of what literature will be like when Microsoft finally rules the world.

Contributors

Sandra Alland is a writer, performer, photographer, and small press fanatic. Her first collection of poetry was *Proof of a Tongue* (McGilligan, 2004).

Margaret Atwood has been published in over forty countries. She is the author of more than thirty works which include fiction, poetry and critical essays. She lives in Toronto with writer Graeme Gibson.

Leanne Averbach is a text and performance artist. In 2005 she released the poetry collection *fever* (Mansfield) and the spoken word-jazz/blues fusion CD *FEVER & Indigo*. Leanne lives in Vancouver and New York. www.leanneaverbach.com

Margaret Avison has won the Governor General's Award for Poetry twice (1960, 1989), the Griffin Prize for Poetry once (2003), and the Canadian Authors Association Poetry Award once (2003). She was born in Galt, Ontario, in 1918 and lives in Toronto.

Kemeny Babineau is editor and publisher of Laurel Reed Books. He has published numerous chapbooks, and has appeared in several anthologies. He lives near Brantford, Ontario, with his wife and two children.

Elizabeth Bachinsky is the author of two collections of poetry: *Curio* (BookThug, 2005) and *Home of Sudden Service* (Nightwood, 2006). She is writer-in-residence for the communities of Maple Ridge and Pitt Meadows, BC.

Nelson Ball is a poet and bookseller living in Paris, Ontario. From 1967 to 1971, he published three bill bissett books (Weed Flower). In 2004 Ball released the collection *At the Edge of the Frog Pond* (Mercury).

Douglas Barbour is the author of many books of poetry and criticism. He is a professor emeritus in the Department of English, University of Alberta.

John Barlow has recorded one CD (*The UFOs of South Toronto*), authored three collections of poetry, produced hundreds of "homemades" and photocopy-magazines and distributed thousands of free handouts.

Rhonda Batchelor has worked in around Canadian publishing as a writer, editor, publisher, bookseller and consultant since 1977. Her books include *Bearings* (Brick), *Interpreting Silence* and *Weather Report* (Beach Holme).

Jill Battson is a "poetry activist" and the author of *Hard Candy* and *Ashes Are Bone and Dust* (Insomniac). She has created and produced many poetry events including her current reading series, "The Poets' Refuge."

Karen Bissenden lives and writes in Salmon Arm, BC.

George Bowering has written over forty titles of poetry and fiction, and has won the Governor General's Award both for poetry (1969) and fiction (1980). He was appointed Canada's first Parliamentary Poet Laureate in 2002.

Di Brandt was shortlisted for the Griffin and Trillium Prizes for her collection *Now You Care* (Coach House, 2003). She recently accepted a Canada Research Chair in Creative Writing at Brandon University, Manitoba. www.dibrandt.ca

Alice Breeze lives and writes in Brisco, BC. She performs one-woman shows and stages plays with children in theatre workshops.

Brian Brett is the author of ten books and a CD. His novel *Coyote* (Thistledown, 2003) was followed by *Uproar's Your Only Music* (Exile, 2004), a memoir in poetry and prose. www.brianbrett.ca

Elizabeth Brewster was born in New Brunswick but since 1972 has lived in Saskatoon, where she is Professor Emeritus at the University of Saskatchewan. She has published five books of fiction, two volumes of autobiography and nineteen collections of poetry.

Allan Briesmaster was the primary organizer of Toronto's Art Bar Poetry Series through most of the 1990s to 2002. He has published five books of his own poetry and is the main literary editor for Seraphim Editions.

Jim Brown met bill at UBC in the mid-'60s, when Brown was co-editor of *Talon* Magazine. An alliance with bill, Seymour Mayne and Patrick Lane spawned the co-operative publishing entity Very Stone House.

John Burgess was raised in upstate New York, worked on a survey crew in Montana, taught English in Japan and now lives in Seattle. His first book of poetry is *Punk Poems* (Ravenna, 2005).

Stephen Cain is the author of the poetry collection *American Standard/Canada Dry* (Coach House, 2005). Previous books include *Torontology* (ECW, 2001) and *dyslexicon* (Coach House, 1999). He lives in Toronto.

Steve Clay is the editor and publisher of Granary Books. In 2001 Clay published bill bissett's hand-painted poetry/art book, *lunaria*. Steve lives in New York with his wife and two young daughters.

Mark Cochrane lives in Vancouver, where he teaches writing and literature at Kwantlen University College. He is the author of *Boy Am I* (Wolsak & Wynn, 1995) and *Change Room* (Talon, 2000).

Leonard Cohen is a poet, novelist, songwriter and monk. In 1969, he won the Governor General's Award for *Selected Poems 1956-1968*, but declined it. Born, raised and educated in Montreal, he now lives in Los Angeles.

Judith Copithorne (rebel, innovator, feminist, teacher, writer and poet) was published in the first issue of *blewointment*. She has published several books since and lives in Vancouver.

arthur cravan is the quintessential pseudonym.

j.d. crosato is a rhythmic hip-hop Barthes/bissett inspired word-sound poet. He met bill at the University of Western Ontario in the early '90s. He performs in high school, university and college classrooms.

Lorna Crozier is Chair of the Department of Writing at the University of Victoria. Her books of poetry have won the Governor General's, Pat Lowther and Canadian Authors Association awards. She lives outside of Victoria with Patrick Lane and their two cats.

jwcurry had his first book of poems *Moebius & A Bottle* (blewointment, 1977), penned between the ages of 12 & 16, published by bill. He's authored several hundred publications spanning a wide range of forms, processes and attentions.

j ocean dennie was a fixture on the Toronto spoken word scene for several years. He has produced and hosted the spoken-word radio shows "The Poet Tree" (bill was a guest in 1999) and "BITE."

John Donlan is a poetry editor with Brick Books and a reference librarian at Vancouver Public Library. He is the author of three collections of poetry, with a fourth due from Brick in 2008.

Paul Dutton is a poet, novelist, essayist and oral sound artist whose artistic focus is the fusion of the literary and musical impulses. He has appeared throughout Canada, the US and Europe, solo and in ensemble (The Four Horsemen, CCMC, Five Men Singing).

M.A.C. Farrant is the author of seven collections of satirical and humorous short fiction, most recently *Darwin Alone in the Universe* (Talon, 2003) and a memoir, *My Turquoise Years* (Greystone, 2004). She lives on Vancouver Island.

Cathy Ford has authored books, chapbooks, folios of poetry and long poems. bill bissett published her first book, *Stray Zale* (blewointment, 1975), and one of blewointment's last, *By Violent Means* (1983).

Patrick Friesen is a poet and playwright who frequently collaborates with musicians. He has published such collections as *Blasphemer's Wheel* (Turnstone, 1994), *A Broken Bowl* (Brick, 1997) and *the breath you take from the lord* (Harbour, 2002) www.patrickfriesen.com

Maxine Gadd has published poetry since the early '60s. Her first book, *guns of the west*, was published by blewointment in 1967. Other works include *hochelaga* (blewointment, 1970), and *westerns, lost language* (Coach House, 1981).

Candis Graham (1949–2005), after twenty-five years of writing in the usual way, started creating word-collage poems. She founded InnerSea, a Victorian greeting-card business based on these poems, in 2004.

Heidi Greco lives in the White Rock area. She works as a writer and editor, and is the author of *Rattlesnake Plantain* (Anvil, 2002), a collection of poems.

Jane Eaton Hamilton is a Vancouver photographer and the author of six books, shortlisted for such awards as the BC Book Prize, the VanCity Book Award, the Pat Lowther Award and the Ferro-Grumley Award. www.janeeatonhamilton.com

Lenore Herb also not from ths erth originalee tho th sources uv ths partikular birthing ar 4evr obscurd in mysteree her film work video n dvd work her editing n archival preserving ar both xtraordinaree n mirakulous her vizual composing is amayzing n stirs th senses shes bin working as well 4 a long time on erth as a poetree n visual art organizr n produsr n writr n was in th band sonik horses th comptessa rocks on

Mitch Highfill first met bill at the Sound Poetry Festival in New York, 1980. He is founder and editor of Prospect Books (1983) and *Red Weather Magazine* (1985), coordinator of the New York reading series "The Poetry Project" and the author of four books.

Pauline Holdstock, novelist, short fiction writer and essayist, lives on Vancouver Island. Pauline's novel *Beyond Measure* (Cormorant, 2004) was nominated for a Giller Prize and won the Ethel Wilson BC Book Prize.

Geoff Inverarity is founder/director of the Gulf Islands Poetry Festival. His drama, *Still Life, With Scissors*, won the 2001 CBC/BC Film short screenplay competition, and he was nominated for a Leo for his screenplay *Once Upon a Time on the Beach*.

Ellen S. Jaffe teaches writing and currently works with Learning through the Arts, based at the Royal Conservatory of Music. Her latest book is *Feast of Lights* (Sumach, 2006). She lives in Hamilton, Ontario.

Kedrick James is an independent publisher, festival director, gallery curator and teacher. He's toured internationally as a performer with many poets and jazz musicians. He teaches at UBC in the Department of Language and Literacy Education.

Karl E. Jirgens is the author of four books, the head of the Department of English at the University of Windsor and the long-standing editor-in-chief and publisher of the international journal *Rampike*.

Adeena Karasick is a poet, media-artist and author of six books of poetry and poetic theory, including *The House That Hijack Built* (Talon, 2004). She is professor of Poetry and Cultural/Semiotic Theory at St. John's University in New York. www.adeenakarasick.com

Bob Kasher has worked in publishing and bookselling for over twenty-five years. He's the author of ten books including *Da Kine Sound: Conversations with the People who Make Hawaiian Music*, *Ethnic Toronto* and *The Tarot of Baseball*.

Penn Kemp performs in arts festivals and conferences around the world. Playwright and sound poet, she has produced six plays and eight CDs. She's had more than twenty books of poetry, drama and fiction published. www.pennkemp.ca

Beth Kinar is a wife, mother of two, cardiology technologist, poetry dabbler, friend of bill and patron of poetry. She and her husband host raging poetry parties featuring bill and a gallery of his paintings in their hospitable West Vancouver home.

Tim Lander is a scribbler, and plays the whistle round the streets. Doesn't have a busker's licence. Books include *Street Heart Poems, The Glass Book* (Ekstasis, 1999), *The Book of Prejudices* and thirty odd chapbooks.

Patrick Lane is the author of over twenty books of poetry, and has received many awards for his writing including the Governor General's Award and the Canadian Authors Association Award for Poetry. Lane lives near Victoria, BC, with poet Lorna Crozier.

Scott Lawrance is a poet currently living on an island up the coast. He met bill and many others in the village of Vancouver in the mid-'60s. Scott appeared frequently in *blewointment* magazine, and bill published *Apocolips* (blewointment, 1967).

d.a. levy (1942–1968), poet, artist, book-artist, and publisher, was a major underground literary figure in Cleveland's poetry/alternative press scene of the 1960s. blewointment published *Zen Concrete* in 1968, the same year he took his own life at the age of twenty-six.

Carol Malyon has authored eight books. In the 1980s she owned the Beaches Book Shop in Toronto. For years she and bill took turns using apartments in Toronto, Vancouver and London, Ontario. She currently lives and writes in Toronto.

Steve McCaffery is a poet and scholar. He was twice nominated for a Governor General's Award, once for *Theory of Sediment* (1991) and the second time for *Seven Pages Missing* (2000). He currently holds the Gray Chair at SUNY Buffalo (Amherst).

Kay McCracken is co-founder of the Shuswap Lake International Writers' Festival in Salmon Arm, BC. Prior, she owned and managed Reflections, a bookstore in Salmon Arm.

Susan McMaster has published poetry, wordmusic collections and scripts, and recordings. She organized the millennial project *Convergence: Poems for Peace*, which brought poetry and art from across Canada to Parliament Hill.

Diana McMullin – "ths pome was beautifulee writtn 4 n abt me in 1988 by diana mcmullin n given 2 me by diana iuv kept it as a tresyur evr sins framd n heer with me"

Marianne Micros is a poet and teaches Renaissance literature and creative writing at the University of Guelph. Her poetry books include *Upstairs Over the Ice Cream* (Ergo, 1979), *The Key of Dee* (Pendas, 2004), and *Seventeen Trees*.

Jay MillAr is a poet, bookseller, publisher (BookThug) and editor. He is the author of three books including *False Maps for Other Creatures* (blewointment, 2005). He lives in Toronto with his wife Hazel and their two boys Reid and Cole.

gustave morin is a werewolf and a ferris wheel, the maker of 'a few poetry' and the author of some five books in and out of print, most recently *The Etcetera Barbecue* (BookThug, 2006). He has been a stalwart champion of the work of bill bissett since 1989, when he first encountered evidence of bissett's truly heroic efforts…

Wendy Morton is an insurance investigator by day, a poet by night. Each Friday night, she hosts Mocambopo, a poetry event in Victoria now in its ninth year. Her books include *Private Eye* (Ekstasis, 2001) and *Undercover* (Ekstasis, 2003).

Susan Musgrave has been shortlisted four times for the Governor General's Award and has received awards in five different categories of writing: poetry, fiction, non-fiction, personal essay, children's writing and for her work as editor.

Brian Nation grew up in Montreal, quit school and hit the road in 1962. In 1963 he passed through Vancouver in time for the Vancouver Poetry Conference where he met and formed a lifelong association with mr bill bissett. www.boppin.com.

Sharon H. Nelson is the author of nine books of poems, and of essays, plays, political analyses and literary reviews. Her essay "A Just Measure: breath, line, body in the work of bill bissett," appears in *The Capilano Review* #23, 1997. www3.sympatico.ca/sharon.nelson

bpNichol (1944–1988) was born in Vancouver. During his lifetime, Nichol published many chapbooks and works which challenged or redefined ideas of texts, books, genres and writing, including *The Martyrology*. He received the Governor General's Award in 1970.

P.K. Page is the award-winning author of many books including ten volumes of poetry, a novel, selected short stories, a screenplay, three books for children and a memoir. Born in England in 1916 and raised on the Canadian prairies, Page resides in Victoria, BC.

Hilary Peach is a poet who marries song to the textures and dynamics of language and physical theatre. She has performed internationally for fifteen years and released her debut CD, *Poems Only Dogs Can Hear*, in 2003.

Carl Peters is the author of *Annotations & Astonishments* (Talon) and *Textual Vishyuns: The Paintings of bill bissett* (Talon). His essay on bissett, "A Writing Inside Writing" (2004), redefined bill's extensive literary contributions.

Jeff Pew is co-founder of Poetry on the Rocks, an annual celebration of spoken word in the east Kootenays. He is a high school counsellor and teaches creative writing. Jeff lives with Alison and their two boys, Kalum and Noah, in Kimberley, BC.

Ross Priddle is a homedad, sound and concrete poet, as well as publisher and editor of *hat* zine. bentspoon.blogspot.com/

Jamie Reid was a member of the collective that began *TISH*, the Vancouver poetry newsletter which also included George Bowering, David Dawson, Frank Davey and Fred Wah. Jamie's most recent book is *I. Another. The Space Between* (Talon, 2004).

Randy Resh is a poet and producer. Through Bigmouth Media, he promotes performance poetry via live events, video, broadcast and multimedia. He is also co-director of Pteros Gallery Toronto, which represents the visual works of mr bissett.

Linda Rogers is an award-winning writer, teacher, broadcaster and past president of the League of Canadian Poets and the Federation of BC Writers. She edited and contributed to *bill bissett, Essays on His Works* (Guernica, 2002).

Joe Rosenblatt was born in Toronto in l933. He has authored more than a dozen books of poetry and fiction, and won the Governor General's and BC Book awards for poetry. He lives in Qualicum Beach with his wife Faye and their four cats.

Stuart Ross is a Toronto writer and small-presser. His most recent books are *Hey, Crumbling Balcony!* (ECW, 2003), *Surreal Estate: 13 Canadian Poets Under the Influence* (Mercury, 2004) and *Confessions of a Small Press Racketeer* (Anvil, 2005). www.hunkamooga.com

Mari-Lou Rowley is a Vancouver poet and science writer. She has published five poetry collections and recorded the CD *Cellular Logic*. In September 2004 she was one of two Canadian poets – with bill bissett – to perform at Seattle's Bumbershoot Festival.

Stephen Roxborough (aka roxword) has published two chapbooks and a spoken word CD, *spiritual demons* (2002). He is co-founder of Burning Word poetry festival, a board member of the Washington Poets Association and Head Poet for Madrona Center.

Sharon Thesen is a BC-based author of ten books of poetry. Former editor of *The Capilano Review* (78–89), Thesen now teaches at UBC Okanagan in Kelowna. Her most recent poetry collection is *The Good Bacteria* (Anansi, 2006).

Yvonne Trainer has published four collections of poetry and given hundreds of readings. Her books include *Tom Three Persons* (Frontenac, 2002) and *Landscape Turned Sideways* (Goose Lane, 1988).

Tom Walmsley is the author of three collections of poetry, seven plays, three novels and one screenplay. He won the inaugural Three Day Novel contest with *Doctor Tin* (Pulp Press, 1979). Born in Liverpool, England, Tom now lives in Toronto.

Ann Walsh is a short story writer, novelist, poet and anthology editor. She's authored seven novels for young adults, many nominated for awards. She has also written a collection of poetry, *Across the Stillness* (Beach Holme, 1993).

Michael Dylan Welch is vice-president of the Haiku Society of America, director of the Haiku North America and Poets in the Park conferences. Originally from England, he now lives with his wife and baby in Sammamish, Washington.

Darren Wershler-Henry is a writer, critic and former editor at Coach House Books. He has two books of poetry, *Nicholodeon: a book of lowerglyphs* and *the tapeworm foundry,* shortlisted for the Trillium Prize. Born in Winnipeg, he now lives in Toronto.

sheri-d wilson is a poet, playwright, filmmaker, essayist, teacher, producer and internationally renowned performer. She has published six collections of poetry and is the artistic director of the Calgary International Spoken Word Festival. www.sheridwilson.com

rox, jeff and bill raging in the raven castle (october, 2005). Photo by Brian Nation.

Acknowledgements

thanks to bill for being bill and letting the whole projekt unfold as it did; Adeena Karasick who agreed to meet a complete stranger; Jamie Reid who unflinchingly spread word of Projekt bill through his extensive network; Sharon Nelson for her brilliant essay on bill ("A Just Measure: breath, line, body in the work of bill bissett"); Pilsner Urquell for its immaculate structure in any underground parkade; Dr. Carl Peters for his dedication, insight and introducing us to Special Collections at SFU; Andy, Colin & the smartest monkeys from Swindon; The Sylvia Hotel for being there, overlooking English Bay on the edge of Stanley Park; Jeff Pew for buddhaful encouragement, sharp editing skill and fabulous Poetry on the Rocks; gustave morin for his xcellent briefings on poetics; Lenore Herb for her dedication to bill, his heart and art; Steve Clay for the exquisite publication of *lunaria*; Falafel King on Denman for pitas full of pleasure; Eric L. Swanick and Lynn Copeland for helpful attention and assistance at SFU Special Collections; Beth, Richard, Mallory and Conner Kinar for hosting raging poetry parties; Jo at StarBar; Maxine Gadd & Judith Copithorne for raging with us at the Kootenay School of Writing; Doug Smith, our bossman at the Stanley Theatre, for his laughter and lightness; to Buk: all our pilsners, cheap wine and longshots; Diana McMullin who escaped ungoogled; Captain Carol for sending her last bissett *Cap Review*; shattered litre mugs at Checkers; Elizabeth Brewster for celebrating her 82nd birthday on the phone with us; Jack Kerouac for knowing enough to call bill "a great poet" (*The Paris Review*, issue 43, 1968); sheri-d for her unswerving support; Kimberley and its fine, albeit thin, oxygen; Guinness, Beckett and Yeats; Paul Dutton for unyielding dedication to the perfect lipogram; Stuart Ross and Heidi Fleiss for championing the third wave and coming to our defence more than once; the vineyards of Chile and Alexander Valley for earthiness, clarity and eventual lubrication; Stephen Roxborough who, 25 years ago, opened a door; Joanne Bellanger for reviving poetry in the Kootenays; Warren Tallman for calling bill "a brave new spirit"; Ladybird, when wood was warm and splintered time; Sean Smith at York University Archives; Leanne Campbell who, over a glass of red, works wonders; Bella Pizza for the best damn pie in Vancouver; the infinite circle of swamis; Ellie Nichol for giving us permission to borrow some of Barrie's genius; Suan Mok Monastery and the twilight chant of crickets; James Reaney for calling bill's blewointment empire "a one-man civilization"; Stanley Park for endless wonder and countless expeditions and reunions; The Old Baurenhaus for a brilliant soup and dumpling dinner with bill; the two Peggys; Milo Duffin for xcellence in design and mixology; The Railway Club for welcoming bums like us as pseudo-members and kicking us out at 4am; d.a.levy for smudging and nudging and blurring the lines of correctness; to our old friend Tom Walmsley for keeping us honest with threats of imaginary violence; the eternal echo of The Four Horsemen; jwcurry who never fell asleep on the phone, despite the hour; the brewmaster monks of Chimay; Tim Lander, a craftsman with needle, thread and chapbook; Lisa Doyle for her steadfast friendship and patience; the fields of laughing bamboo; Alison, Kalum and Noah Ko for waiting and smiling; Zachary and Eli Roxborough for their boundless love and youth; Silas White and Kathy Sinclair for embracing the vision to honour bill; all the poets who spread the word and conjured poetic offerings with an overwhelming, unconditional generosity of spirit; and most importantly, billyuns uv thankx again to bill bissett, without whom this cosmic portrait and celebration would not be possible.

i was inatelee   i thot wanting 2 b a ballet danser
n a figure skatr at 10 i startid what wud b almost 2 yeers uv
abdominal operaysyns 4 peritinitis 12 ops   in th oxygen tent i assessd
realizd i cud nevr attain aeithr uv my ambishyuns
as th abdominal muskul wall was 4evr messd up cut thru etsetera
n thn it ocurrd 2 me that i cud write n paint n that
way letting th words n images danse play on th papr
whatevr th surface canvas wood i wud stil thn b always involvd in th
kreeaysyun uv moovment fluiditee danses   thees second choices bcame
inate first choices   n prhaps they had bin all along   xcellent

advise 2 aspiring writirs   write as much a spossibul howevr n
whatevr yu want   ar led 2   n b aware uv yr own possibul self
censoring in all wayze n b wanting 2 let go uv that thos urges

                    bill bissett   novembr 2005

```
memo
  i
will
  really
disappear
  once
```

–bill bissett
we sleep inside each other all

Publication Credits

Nelson Ball	"I've Never Seen a Mountain" from *With Issa: Poems 1964-1971* (ECW Press, 1991)
bill bissett	"bare bones biography what els shudint i remember" from *NOBODY OWNS TH EARTH* (Anansi, 1971)
George Bowering	"bill bissett" from *Curious* (Coach House, 1973)
Elizabeth Brewster	"Gold Man" from *Sunrise North* (Clarke, Irwin, 1974)
Allan Briesmaster	"bill bissett" from *Phantelles* (Aeolus House, 2003)
Jim Brown	"The bissetts" from *If There Are Any Noahs* (Talonbooks, 1968); "Th Very Tissues of Language" (blewointment press, Volume 5, No. 2, Aug, 1968)
Stephen Cain	"bill bissett" from *dyslexicon* (Coach House, 1999)
Mark Cochrane	"Sexing the Page" from *Change Room* (Talonbooks, 2000)
arthur cravan	"bill bissett re/view" from a broadside (Letters, 1980s)
jwcurry	"Review of Th gossamer bed pan" from *RE: VIEWS: RE: SPONSES* (Jumbo Plums, 1987); reprinted/revised (Runaway Spoon Press, 1991)
John Donlan	"Shedden" from *Poetry Canada*, 10(2), summer 1989
d.a.levy	"Dream Yoga Techniques" from *Zen Concrete* (blewointment, 1968)
Carol Malyon	"illuminaysyun" from *Colville's People* (The Mercury Press, 2002)
Jay MillAr	excerpt from "No. 9 of the small blue" from *the small blue* (BookThug, 2003)
Susan Musgrave	"We Come This Way But Once" from *What the Small Day Cannot Hold* (Beach Holme, 2000)
bpNichol	excerpt from "Book of Common Prayer" from *The Martyrology Book 2* (Coach House, 1972) "a pome by bill bissett" from *As Elected, Selected Writing* (Talonbooks, 1980)
Jamie Reid	"biseteez" from *I. Another. The Space Between: Selected Poems* (Talonbooks, 2004)
Darren Wershler-Henry	"Nightmare Anthology: The Corrected bill bissett" from *Nicholodeon: a book of lowerglyphs* (Coach House, 1997)
sheri-d wilson	"Re:rejoice in blue hat bill" from *Re:Zoom* (Frontenac House, 2005)